Big
Bad
Classroom
Jokes

Big Bad Classroom Jokes

Sandy Ransford

Robinson Children's Books

Robinson Publishing Ltd
7 Kensington Church Court
London
W8 4SP

First published in the UK by Robinson Children's Books,
an imprint of Robinson Publishing Ltd, 1998

This collection © Robinson Publishing Ltd, 1998
Illustrations © David Mostyn, 1998

A copy of the British Library Cataloguing in Publication Data for this
title is available from the British Library.

ISBN 1 85487 631 7

Printed and bound in the EC

10 9 8 7 6 5 4 3 2 1

Contents

Introduction

Do you enjoy school, or do you only like it in the holidays when it's closed? Either way, I'll bet you enjoy laughing about it! So here's your chance. This book contains over 1,000 jokes about everything connected with school, including classes and subjects, teachers and pupils, exams and absences, games and break time, meals and treats, even holidays! Whether you want to tease your friends or make fun of your teachers, to store up jokes to enliven even the dullest lesson, or simply to have a cracking good laugh at break time, you should find plenty to amuse you within these pages. Listen. The bell's gone (who stole it?), and it's time to begin today's lessons. With this book in your pocket you should be safe from boredom, and guaranteed to learn a lot!

Start of Term

Jimmy had just come home after his very first day at school.
"How did you enjoy your first day in the classroom?" asked his dad.
"First day?" asked Jimmy. "Do you mean I have to go back again tomorrow?"

After he'd been at school a week, Jimmy's dad again asked him how he was getting on.
"Do you get on well with the teacher?" he asked.
"Oh, yes," replied Jimmy. "I think she likes me."
"Why's that?" asked his dad.
"She puts kisses on all of my sums."

What must you pay when you go to school?
Attention.

Fifth grade pupils were asked to draw a picture of the Holy Family's flight into Egypt.
George drew a picture of an airplane, containing Mary, Joseph and Jesus and a fourth person. Their teacher decided to ignore the airplane and explain later what "flight" meant, but she asked George who the fourth person was.
"Oh," replied the lad, "that's Pontius the pilot."

"Why were you sent home from school?" asked
Micky's mom.
"Because the boy next to me was smoking,"
answered Micky.
"But if he was smoking why were you sent home?"
"It was me who set him on fire."

Molly was sent to the principal's study.
"Your teacher has been complaining about you,"
said the principal. "What have you been doing?"
"Nothing, Miss," replied Molly.
"I guessed as much," said the principal grimly.

TEACHER: What's the matter, Alison?
ALISON: I shut my fumb in the door, Miss.
TEACHER: It's "thumb," Alison, not "fumb."
ALISON: Yes, Miss. And I shut my thinger in as well.

TEACHER: What comes after G?
ANNABEL: Whiz.
TEACHER: I don't think you understand me. Let's
try again. What comes after U?
ANNABEL: My mom if I don't tidy my room.
TEACHER (sighing): Oh dear. Let's try one more
time. What comes after T?
ANNABEL: Supper!

TEACHER: If I bought twenty-five buns for $1 what would each one be?
RILEY: Stale, Miss.

TEACHER: Your writing is terrible, Andrew. That 7 looks like a 9.
ANDREW: It is a 9, Sir.
TEACHER: Then why does it look like a 7?

The math teacher was trying to teach her class about decimals. She wrote 25.8 on the blackboard and then rubbed out the decimal point to show what happened when you multiply by ten.
"Where is the decimal point now?" she asked.
Lucy put up her hand. "On the duster," she replied.

When Maureen told her mother she'd been banned from cookery classes her mother asked why.
"I burned something," said Maureen.
"That doesn't sound too serious," said her mother. "What did you burn?"
"I burned the classroom down," explained poor Maureen.

TEACHER: Why was the period before 1200 AD called the Dark Ages?
OLLIE: Because there were so many knights.

What was King Arthur's favorite game?
Knights and crosses.

Why did King Arthur have a round table?
So no one could corner him.

MAGGIE (sighing): I wish I'd been born hundreds of years ago.
MILLY: Why's that?
MAGGIE: I wouldn't have had so much history to learn!

Why is history like a fruit loaf?
It's full of dates.

FATHER: Math was my best subject at school. I don't understand why your marks are so poor.
FREDDIE: But I did get nine out of ten.
FATHER: Yes, but 50 percent isn't good enough.

$$\begin{array}{r} 3467 \\ +\,9876 \\ \hline 13343 \end{array}$$

TEACHER: If you add 3,467 and 9,876 what do you get?
TILLY: The wrong answer.

TEACHER: If I gave you four rabbits today, and tomorrow gave you another five rabbits, how many rabbits would you have?
TANIA: Ten.
TEACHER: How do you make it ten?
TANIA: I've already got one at home.

Who invented algebra?
An X-pert.

The class was having trouble sorting out difficult words, so the teacher said, "Who can tell me the difference between pneumonia and ammonia?" Smarty-pants Andy answered, "One comes in chests; the other in bottles."

TEACHER: How many letters are there in the alphabet?
SMARTY-PANTS ANDY: Eleven.
TEACHER: Eleven?
SMARTY-PANTS ANDY: Yes: T, H, E, A, L, P, H, A, B, E, T.

BILLY: What Shakespeare play are you studying?
WILLY: I call it *Julius, Grab the Girl Before She Escapes*.
BILLY: Eh?
WILLY: It's usually called *Julius Caesar*.

The teacher was trying to find out how many of her pupils in the new intake could read and write. She asked young Barbara.
"I can write," replied Barbara, "but I can't read."
"Write your name for me," said the teacher, handing the girl a piece of paper and a pencil. Barbara scribbled something and gave it back.
"What does this say?" asked the teacher.
"I don't know," replied Barbara. "I can't read."

SAM: Mom, can you write in the dark?
MOM: I should think so, why?
SAM: Will you sign this school report, please?

HETTIE: What are you reading?
BETTY: A book about electricity.
HETTIE: Current events?
BETTY: No, just light reading.

TEACHER: Where are you from, Owen?
OWEN: Wales, Miss.
TEACHER: Which part?
OWEN: All of me, Miss.

TEACHER: Who can tell me the difference between "like" and "love"?
CAROL: I can, Miss. I like my mom and dad, but I love chocolate toffees.

GORDON: Would you punish someone for something they hadn't done?
TEACHER: No, of course not.
GORDON: Oh, good, because I haven't done my homework.

TEACHER: Why are you late this time, Jenkins?
JENKINS: I broke my ankle, Sir.
TEACHER: That's a lame excuse.

TEACHER: If I say "I have went" you know it's wrong, don't you?
SALLY: Yes, Miss, because you ain't went, you're still here.

What's the most popular answer to a teacher's questions?
"I don't know."

ANGRY TEACHER: I thought I told you to stand at the end of the line!
KEVIN: I did, Sir, but there was someone there already!

Mervyn was the school swot. He'd killed more flies than anyone else at the school.

Why did King Henry VIII have so many wives?
He liked to chop and change.

TEACHER: Harold! When you yawn you should put
your hand in front of your mouth!
HAROLD: What, and get it bitten?

TEACHER: How many
famous people were born
in Roman times?
CLEVER CLARENCE: None,
Sir, they were all babies.

TEACHER: What was the Romans'
greatest achievement?
HENRY: Learning Latin!

FIRST ROMAN SOLDIER: What's the time?
SECOND ROMAN SOLDIER: XX past III.

TEACHER: Where can we find the Pyramids?
DARREN: Where the last person to use them left them.

TINA: Why did they build Rome at night, Miss?
TEACHER: What a funny question. What makes you think they built it at night?
TINA: Because Mom is always saying Rome wasn't built in a day.

Why was the little Egyptian girl worried? Because her daddy was a mummy.

What did Egyptian mummies
paint on their fingers when
they went to parties?
Nile varnish.

Henry = $\frac{1}{8}$

Who invented fractions?
King Henry the Eighth.

TEACHER: What was the first thing King
William did on gaining the throne?
NIGEL: Sat down?

TEACHER: Your history marks aren't very good,
Barry.
BARRY: That's because you're always asking me
about things that happened before I was born.

What did one math book say to the other?
"Have I got problems!"

TEACHER: Do you know how to make a fire with two sticks?
JACK: Yes, you make sure one of them is a match.

What do punks learn at school?
Punk-tuation.

ENGLISH TEACHER: Does anyone know what "unaware" means?
NICK: Yes, it's what you put on first thing in the morning.

TEACHER: This essay on "My Dog" is exactly the same as your sister's.
DARREN: Well, it's the same dog, Miss.

TEACHER: Sharon, this essay looks as if it's in your mother's handwriting.
SHARON: I borrowed her pen, Miss.

BILLY: What's your favorite school subject?
MILLY: Gozinta.
BILLY: What do you mean, "gozinta"?
MILLY: You know, two gozinta four, four gozinta eight...

Why is school like a shower?
One wrong turn and you're in hot water.

"Maria, it's time for your violin lesson!"
"Oh, fiddle!"

TEACHER: Jason! Didn't you hear me call you?
JASON: Yes, Sir, but you told me never to answer back.

TEACHER: Alec! Were you copying Andy's work?
ALEC: No, I was just checking that he'd got mine right.

GEOGRAPHY TEACHER: What's the coldest place in the world?
DARREN: Chile?

PHYSICS TEACHER: Light travels at 186,000 miles a second. Isn't that amazing?
ROY: Not really. After all, it's downhill all the way.

Madge arrived at school one day covered in spots. She was sent off to the doctor and asked him, "Do you think I've caught decimals?"

TEACHER: Do you know what the Cheddar Gorge is?
CHARLIE: A very thick cheese sandwich?

ENGLISH TEACHER: Damian, give me a sentence with two pronouns in it.
DAMIAN: Who, me?
ENGLISH TEACHER: Well done!

TEACHER: What's your name?
GEORGE: George.
TEACHER: Say "Sir" when you speak to me.
GEORGE: All right, Sir George.

GILL: My pen's run out.
BILL: You'd better run after it then.

TEACHER: Who signed the Magna Carta?
LETTIE: It wasn't me, Miss!

TEACHER: What's the opposite of "minimum"?
CARRIE: "Minidad"?

MATTIE: Is our school haunted?
HATTIE: I don't think so. Why?
MATTIE: The principal is always talking about the school spirit.

TEACHER: Can you give me an example of a collective noun?
NINA: Er, a vacuum cleaner?

NORMAN: Have you been giving Miss Lamb apples again?
NELLIE: No, why?
NORMAN: I overheard her telling Miss Piglet that you gave her the pip.

TEACHER: Why do birds fly south in winter?
CELIA: It's too far to walk.

TEACHER: What's a centimeter?
MARY: It's an insect with 100 legs.

What's the difference between a good dog and a bad pupil?
One rarely bites; the other barely writes.

SCIENCE TEACHER: What happened when electricity was discovered?
PADDY: I expect someone got a nasty shock.

ROB: After school I've got to go home and cut the lawn.
BOB: Did your father promise you something if you cut it?
ROB: No, but he promised me something if I don't!

SIGN ON THE SCHOOL CARETAKER'S OFFICE: Will the person who took my ladder please return it or further steps will be taken.

What do you get if you cross a caretaker with an elephant?
A heavy-duty cleaner.

SCIENCE TEACHER: Who can explain what a laser is?
LAURIE: It's what a Chinaman shaves with.

What does a music teacher do when he's locked out of the classroom?
Sings until he gets the right key.

TEACHER: What was the *Tyrannosaurus rex*?
JAMIE: A shipwreck?

When the class went on a nature ramble, Monty spotted a grass snake. "Quick!" he shouted, "look at this! It's a tail without a body!"

TEACHER: What do you know about Tunisia?
TOMMY: It's a disease where you lose your memory.

In Class

TEACHER: Stop showing off, Ben. Do you think you're the teacher here?
BEN: No, Sir.
TEACHER: Then stop behaving badly.

TEACHER: Only fools are absolutely sure about things. Wise people hesitate.
KEITH: Are you sure?
TEACHER: I'm certain.

TEACHER: Who can tell me what a synonym is?
BETTY: It's a word you use in place of one you can't spell.

How can you hire the school piano?
Put a book under each of its legs.

Why was the piano teacher
arrested?
Because he got into treble.

What's got eight legs and sings?
The school quartet.

TEACHER: What's the longest
night of the year?
DONALD: A fortnight.

Knock, knock.
Who's there?
Quiet Tina.
Quiet Tina who?
Quiet Tina classroom!

On which side of a school should a rosebush grow?
The outside!

TEACHER: What's the outside of a tree called?
TRACEY: Don't know.
TEACHER: Doesn't anyone know?
CLASS: No, Miss.
TEACHER: Bark, children, bark!
CLASS: Woof! Woof!

STACEY: I was top of the class last week.
TRACEY: How'd you manage that?
STACEY: We had to answer a question about spiders. The teacher asked how many legs they'd got and I said five.
TRACEY: But that wasn't right!
STACEY: No, but it was the nearest anyone got!

Knock, knock.
Who's there?
Alaska.
Alaska who?
Alaska the teacher if I can leave the room.

Knock, knock.
Who's there?
Harmony.
Harmony who?
Harmony times must I tell you not to do that!

TEACHER: Order, children, order!
DAFT DEREK: Two chocolate ice creams and
three orange lollipops, please.

JIMMY: Did Noah really build an ark?
TEACHER: When I get to heaven I'll ask him.
JIMMY: But what if he didn't go to heaven?
TEACHER: Then you can ask him.

PIANO TUNER: I've come to tune the school piano.
PRINCIPAL: But we didn't send for you.
PIANO TUNER: No, but the people who live across
the road did.

TEACHER: Sally, what are you chewing?

SALLY: Gum, Miss.

TEACHER: You were eating toffees on Monday, fruit gums on Tuesday and now it's chewing gum. Why?

SALLY: Because I haven't any toffees or fruit gums left, Miss.

JENNY: My sister goes to a fee-paying school.

KENNY: I'm not surprised. No one would have her unless they were paid!

TEACHER: Your work is dreadful, Sheila. I don't know how it's possible for a person to make as many mistakes in one day as you do!

SHEILA: I get here early, Miss.

MAVIS: Our teacher is like the *Mona Lisa*.

TRAVIS: You mean she smiles a lot?

MAVIS: No, she's so old she should be in a museum!

TEACHER: If you eat any more, Ronald, you'll burst!
RONALD: Then you'd better stand clear, Sir, as I've just had a second helping!

ART TEACHER: I asked you to draw a horse and cart but you've only drawn the horse. Why?
WILLIAM: I thought the horse could draw the cart.

DARREN: I think my drawing is a rare work of art.
ART TEACHER: It's certainly not well done!

ART TEACHER: What colors would you paint the sun and the wind?
DAFT DEREK: The sun rose and the wind blue.

Why are many famous artists Italian?
Because they were born in Italy.

What do you call the famous Italian artist who did his paintings sitting on the fridge?
Bottichilli.

ART TEACHER: What can you tell me about the great Renaissance artists, Carol?
CAROL: Er, they're all dead, Miss.

What did the painting say to the wall?
"First they framed me, then they hung me."

What's the best way to get spilled paint off
your chair?
Sit on it before the paint's dry.

MUSIC TEACHER: Have you finished your piano
practice, Fiona?
FIONA: Yes, Miss. I was playing a duet with
Freddie but I finished first.

MUSIC TEACHER: Your
hands are filthy,
Francesca. You must
wash them before you
play the piano.
FRANCESCA: What if I
promise only to play on
the black notes?

SHARON: Did you really
manage to learn the
piano in six easy
lessons?
MUSIC TEACHER: Yes.
It was the 200 that
came afterwards that
were hard.

SHEILA: How long have you been playing the piano, Miss?
MUSIC TEACHER: Oh, about fifteen years, on and off.
SHEILA: Was the stool slippery?

BOBBIE: Did the music teacher really say you had a heavenly voice?
ROBBIE: Not exactly. She said it was like nothing on earth.

Why is a locked piano hard to open? Because the keys are all on the inside.

Why are pianos noble instruments? Because they're either upright or grand.

What's the best instrument to give a musical child?
A drum takes a lot of beating.

What musical instrument never tells the truth?
A lyre.

Little Alice was given a recorder and a bottle of perfume for her birthday. It made her feel very grown up, so when she went to school she splashed the perfume over herself and took the recorder in her pocket, to practise on during the lunch break. As she sat down for lunch between two of her friends, she giggled and confided, "If you hear a little noise, and smell a little smell, it's me."

Jimmy and Timmy went to boarding school, and when Jimmy's teacher found out Jimmy hadn't been taking a shower each day he was in trouble.
"But how did he find out?" asked Timmy.
"I forgot to dirty my towel," replied Jimmy.

Have you heard the joke about the school bed?
I'm afraid it hasn't been made up yet.

One weekend Sally went to
stay with her friends Susie and
Sarah, and, as there were
other people staying at the
house, they all three had to
sleep in the same bed, which
was a bit crowded.
"Tell you what," said Sally. "I'll
sleep on the floor then you'll
have more room."
After a while Susie tapped
her on the shoulder.
"You can come back in,"
she said, "there's much
more room now."

MATH TEACHER: Cynthia,
please don't hum while
studying your algebra
textbook.
CYNTHIA: I wasn't studying it,
Miss, just humming.

TEACHER: Today we're going
to study energy
conservation. Who can give
me an example of energy
being wasted?
SILLY SUE: Telling a hair-raising
story to a bald man!

As the teacher walked into the classroom it got very noisy, with lots of people all trying to talk to her at once. She raised her hand to try to quell the din, and called out, "Be quiet when you talk to me!"

TEACHER: Who's the monitor this week? Is it you, Harold?
HAROLD: Yes, Miss.
TEACHER: Have you put fresh water in the fish tank?
HAROLD: No, Miss, they haven't drunk the water I gave them yesterday yet.

FLYNN: What's your new crafts teacher like?
LYNN: A sew-and-sew.

FRENCH TEACHER: Who knows what *mal de mer* means?
MARTIN: Is it soreness after riding a horse, sir?

FRENCH TEACHER: What's the French national anthem called?
SILLY SARAH: The Mayonnaise.

What do you call a school jacket that's on fire?
A blazer.

What did the school beret say to the school tie?
"You hang around while I go on ahead."

When does ll plus ll equal lll?
When you can't add up!

Why is it dangerous to add up in a safari
park?
Because if you add u and u you get 8
(ate).

JOHNNY: My teacher thinks I tell lies.
BONNIE: I don't believe you.

TEACHER: Who knows what an Eskimo is?
WITTY WINNIE: One of God's frozen people.

TEACHER: How do you spell "rhinoceros"?
TILLY: R, I, N, O, S, E, R, O, S, S.
TEACHER: That isn't how the dictionary spells it.
TILLY: You didn't ask me how the dictionary
spells it.

ENGLISH TEACHER: Can you give me a sentence
with the word "fascinate" in it?
SALLY: My cardigan's got eleven buttons but I can
only fasten eight.

Did you hear the joke abut the pencil?
There's no point to it.

Knock, knock.
Who's there?
Pencil.
Pencil who?
Pencil fall down if your
elastic breaks!

Why is a classroom like an old car?
It's full of nuts and has a crank at the front.

Two girls were talking quietly at the back of the
class.
"That boy over there really annoys me," said Jenny.
"But he's not even looking at you," answered
Janey.
"I know, that's what's
annoying me,"
said Jenny.

TRICIA: Tina's just swallowed her pen, Miss.
TEACHER: Tell her to use a pencil, then.

When Johnnie went to a new school his new
teacher said, "Haven't I seen your face
somewhere before?"
"I don't think so," replied Johnnie. "It's always
been between my ears!"

KINDERGARTEN TEACHER: What happened when
Humpty Dumpty fell off the wall?
MADGE: All the king's horses and all the king's men
had scrambled eggs for tea.

TEACHER: Who invented the radio?
DOPEY DONALD: Macaroni.

DICK: Have
you heard the
joke about
the dirty shirt?
RICK: No.
DICK: That's
one on you!

What do you get if you
cross the teacher you
like the least with a
telescope?
A horrorscope.

Wally and Molly went round collecting for the school's new swimming pool.
One bright spark offered them a bucketful of water.

TEACHER: Have you ever seen a windowbox?
CLEVERCLOGS CHARLIE: No, but I've seen a garden fence.

TEACHER: Why are you trying to cross the road here? It's dangerous. Can't you see there's a zebra crossing just down there?
WINNIE: Well, I hope it's having better luck than I am!

Why did the teacher give the pupil a "B"?
Because he had hives.

TEACHER: Do you know who Ivanhoe was?
BENNY: Er, a Russian gardener?

Why did the school orchestra have bad manners?
Because it didn't know how to conduct itself.

TEACHER: Write out "I must not be rude to Sammy" 100 times.
CECIL: A hundred times! I was only rude to him once!

TEACHER: In which battle was Lord Nelson killed?
JACK: His last one.

TEACHER: Who knows what a draftsman does?
MICKY: He leaves doors open.

TEACHER: Who knows what we mean by the "Cold War"?
LARRY: Er, a snowball fight?

TEACHER: What do you get if you add 8,136 and 7,257, subtract 93 and divide the answer by 5?
JULIE: A headache.

Knock, knock.
Who's there?
Stu.
Stu who?
Stu late to go to school now!

Play the Game

"Stop the ball!" yelled the sports master. "Stop the ball!"
Little Billy, in goal, was crying.
"What's the matter?" yelled the master.
"Please, sir, isn't that what the goal is for?" snivelled Billy.

What position did the ducks play in the school football team?
Right and left quack.

Why is football like fresh milk?
It strengthens the calves.

How does an octopus go onto a school football pitch?
Well armed!

If you have a referee in football and an umpire in tennis, what do you have in bowls?
Goldfish!

What game can you play with a shopping bag?
Basketball.

HOPELESS HARRY: I've thought of a way of making the school football team more successful.
SPORTS TEACHER: Oh good. Are you leaving it?

What do you call someone who shouts loudly at a soccer match?
A foot-bawler.

Why was Cinderella kicked out of the school football team?
She kept running away from the ball.

"How should I have played that last shot?" the young tennis player asked his coach. "Under an assumed name," he replied.

Why is tennis such a noisy game? Because every player raises a racket.

BETTY: I think tennis is a rich person's game.
HETTIE: Nonsense! Look at all the poor players!

Why should a golfer wear two pairs of trousers?
In case he gets a hole in one.

Susie
and Sally
were talking about swimming
and their friend Selma.
"She's a baby swimmer," said Susie.
"Why do you call her that?" asked Sally.
"She's eight years old."
"Because," replied Susie, "she can only crawl."

Milly was old enough to worry about her weight.
"I think I must do more swimming," she said. "I've heard that's a good way to keep slim."
"It can't be," replied her friend Maggie. "Have you ever noticed the shape of a whale?"

Is it dangerous to swim on a full stomach?
Well, it's better to swim in water!

What goes in pink and comes out blue?
A swimmer in winter!

How can you swim 100 meters in a few seconds?
Go over a waterfall!

Did you hear about the loony who tried to swim
across Lake Ontario?
When he was 50 meters from the far side he decided he was too tired to continue so he turned
round and went back the way he'd come.

DONG

When is a swimming
costume like a bell?
When you wring it out.

Class 4 went out on a hike and their teacher was trying to make them understand how to read maps and points of the compass.

"If you face north," he said, "what's on your right?"

"East," replied Harry.

"Right!" said the teacher. "And what's on your left?"

"West," replied Larry.

"Right again," said the teacher. "And what's behind you?"

"The rucksack with my lunch in it," replied Barry.

Bill and Ben were walking past a house when the owner ran out.

"Oi," he shouted, "is this your ball?"

Bill looked at Ben.

"Er, has it done any damage?" Ben asked the man.

"No," he replied.

"Then it's ours," said Bill.

ANDY: I have a chance on the baseball team.

MANDY: I didn't even know they were raffling it.

Jan and Stan were having their first baseball lesson.

"How do you hold the bat?" asked Jan.

"By the wings," replied Stan.

CHARLIE: Were you any good at school sports, Dad?
DAD: I once ran 100 meters in two seconds. And if I ever find out who put those ants in my shorts I'll shoot him!

What did the world's worst athlete do? Ran a bath and came in second!

How do you start a jelly race? Say, "Get set!"

How do you start a milk pudding race? Sago!

Why is a football stadium cool?
It's full of fans.

How many people can you fit into the world's largest empty sports stadium?
One. After that it isn't empty any more.

Bertie was sent home from school to collect his sports kit for games that afternoon. When he returned he was wet through.
"Whatever's happened to you?" asked his teacher.
"You told me I had to wear my sports kit for games this afternoon," replied Bertie, "but it was all in the wash."

BERNIE: The teacher said I could play in the school football team if it weren't for two things.
ERNIE: What are they?
BERNIE: My feet.

"Sorry I missed that goal," said
Teddy to his captain.
"I could kick myself."
"Don't try," said the captain,
"you'd miss."

BERYL: My dog plays tennis.
CHERYL: He must be very clever.
BERYL: He's not that
clever, I nearly
always win.

DONNIE: I dream about football every night.
JOHNNIE: Don't you ever dream about girls?
DONNIE: What, and miss a chance at goal?

Why didn't the loony go water-skiing?
He couldn't find a lake that sloped.

Why wouldn't the loony play water polo?
He couldn't ride a horse.

What's the hardest thing about learning to ride a horse?
The ground!

SALLY: I went riding at the weekend.
WALLY: Horseback?
SALLY: Yes, he got back about an hour before me.

Gemma went with Emma to the riding stables, and waited while Emma went out for a ride. When she returned she was covered in mud. "What happened?" asked Gemma. "You know where the track forks on the common?" asked Emma. Gemma nodded. "I wanted to go to the right and the horse wanted to go to the left." "And did he win?" asked Gemma. "Well, we tossed for it," replied her friend.

Ted and Fred were enjoying themselves in the snow.
"You can borrow my sledge if you like," said Ted.
"Thanks," said Fred. "We'll share it, shall we?"
"Yes," said Ted. "I'll have it going downhill and you can have it going uphill."

How long does it take to learn to skate?
A few sittings!

Why do little boys play football?
For kicks.

How do you stop moles digging up the sports ground?
Hide their spades.

Why was the snowman no good at playing in the big match?
He got cold feet.

GLEN: Do you have holes in your gym shorts?
KEN: No.
GLEN: Then how do you get your legs in them?

Why was the centipede late for the match?
He was lacing up his boots.

Who runs out on to the pitch when a player is injured and says, "Miaow"?
The first-aid kit.

What did the left football boot say to the right football boot?
"Between us we should have a ball."

MOM: Did you get into a fight at the match again? You've lost your front teeth!
PETE: No I haven't, they're in my pocket.

FIRST MOM: What position does your son play in the school football team?
SECOND MOM: I think he's one of the drawbacks.

How do you stop someone who's been working out in the gym on a hot day from smelling?
Put a peg on his nose!

Two fans were waiting to get into the big match.
"Are you superstitious?" asked the first.
"No," replied the second.
"In that case," said the first, "give me $13 for the entrance money."

Mrs Feather realized that her neighbor was a famous sportsman.
"I've seen you on the television, on and off," she said.
"And how do you like me?" asked the sportsman.
"Off," replied Mrs Feather.

Knock, knock.
Who's there?
Willy.
Willy who?
Willy score?
Bet he won't!

Knock, knock.
Who's there?
General Lee.
General Lee who?
General Lee I go swimming, but today I'm playing basketball.

Knock, knock.
Who's there?
Canoe.
Canoe who?
Canoe come out and play
ball?

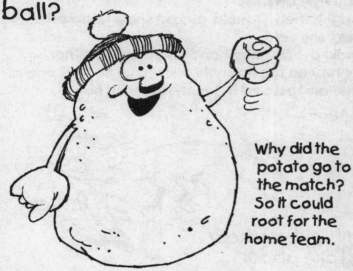

Why did the
potato go to
the match?
So it could
root for the
home team.

John's school team were trying to get into the top
league. "I'm sure we can do it," said John. "All we
have to do is win six of our next three matches."

Class 4B were doing exercises in the gym. "Next,"
said the teacher, "lie down on your backs and
bend and stretch your legs in the air as if you were
riding a bicycle. Jenny, why aren't you pedalling?"
"I'm freewheeling, Miss."

The gym teacher was trying to teach the class how to do handstands, and no one was very good at it.

"Can anyone here stand on their hands?" she asked.

"I can, Miss," said Donald.

The teacher looked doubtful. Donald was rather a tubby little boy.

"All right, then, Donald, please show us how it's done," she said.

Donald put first one hand and then the other carefully on the floor, then lifted up his feet one at a time and placed them on top of his hands.

DAN: Did you hear the joke about the rope?
ANNE: No.
DAN: Oh, skip it!

How short can gym shorts get?
They'll always be above two feet.

Why was the biggest boy in the class put on a diet as well as made to do more exercises?
Because he was thick to his stomach.

Bill and Ben went swimming in the river, and Ben, who was not a very good swimmer, got into difficulties. As he was desperately trying to keep afloat, Bill shouted, "Ben, if you drown can I have your bike?"

How can you jump over two men sitting down?
Play checkers.

Who won the milk drinking contest?
The cat.
How?
It lapped the field.

Did you hear about the
two fat boys
who ran a
race?
One ran
in short
bursts;
the other in
burst shorts.

What kind of schoolboy can jump higher than a house?
All kinds — houses can't jump!

Why did the canoeist take a water pistol with him?
So he could shoot the rapids.

What does a rower drink at bedtime?
Oar-licks.

Why did the girl who
was learning to sail
always carry a bag of
raisins with her?
So if she got into
difficulty the currants
would carry her
ashore.

What kind of leather makes the best football boots?
I don't know, but banana peel makes the best slippers.

What runs around all day and lies down at night with its tongue hanging out?
A training shoe.

Why is a pair of much worn training shoes like a cab driver?
They both drive you away.

Behind the
Bike Shed

Two little boys were having a fight in the
playground when a teacher caught them.
"Now then," he said, "you know the rules here.
No fighting allowed."
"But we weren't fighting aloud," said one boy.
"We were fighting very quietly!"

Little Johnny had also been fighting and his
teacher said, "Johnny! Didn't I tell you to count to
ten so you wouldn't lose your temper?"
"Yes, Miss," sighed Johnny. "But Harry's teacher
only told him to count up to five and he hit me first."

"Boys, boys!" cried the teacher, discovering yet
another scrap going on. "Didn't I tell you not to
fight? You must learn to give and take!"
"That's what he did," sniffed Jerry. "He took my
football and gave me a black eye!"

Did you hear that a large hole has been
discovered in the school playground? Surveyors
are looking into it.

Darren, who was rather fond of Sharon, gave her a box of chocolates at break time on her birthday. "Here you are," he said, blushing, "sweets to the sweet."
"Oh, thanks," said Sharon. "Have a nut."

What happens if you eat too many sweets?
You take up two seats in the bus!

How can you stop a lollipop from slipping out of your mouth?
Grit your teeth.

Knock, knock.
  Who's there?
    Felix.
      Felix who?
        Felix my lollipop again I'll
          bash him!

What did the toffee bar say to the lollipop?
"Hello, sucker!"

What favorite chocolate treat is found on the seabed?
An oyster egg.

What's chocolate on the outside, peanuts on the inside and sings hymns?
A Sunday school treet.

The teachers have a coffee break in the middle of each morning. One said, "Ugh, this coffee tastes like mud!"
"Well," replied another, "it was ground just a few moments ago."

What do vampires have in the middle of each morning?
A coffin break.

Naughty
Nova
nipped
out
one
break time to
visit the local shop.
She asked, "Have you any broken biscuits?"
"Yes," replied the shopkeeper.
"Then you shouldn't be so clumsy," said Nova cheekily.

Why was the biscuit unhappy? Because its mother had been a wafer so long.

What did the biscuits say to the walnuts?
"You're nuts and we're crackers!"

What did the biscuit say
when its friend crossed the
road?
"Oh, crumbs!"

What's lemonade?
Helping an old lemon across the road.

TINA: This milk is very watery.
MONITOR: I expect the cow must have been out
in the rain.

What happened at the milking competition?
Udder chaos.

Why are card games popular at school?
Because whoever plays them holds hands.

BOB: Why have you stopped playing cards with Bill?
ROB: Would you play cards with someone who always cheats?
BOB: No.
ROB: Neither will Bill!

When is a chess player happiest?
When he takes a knight off.

Where can you buy a secondhand chess set?
At a pawnbroker's.

What's a crocodile's favorite game?
Snap!

Did you hear about the bicycle that went around biting people?
It was known as the vicious cycle.

A pupil knocked into an old lady while out riding his bike.
"Look out!" she cried. "Don't you know how to ride a bike?"
"Yes," replied the boy. "But I haven't yet learned how to ring the bell!"

Bill and Ben rode a tandem bicycle, and while they were going uphill Bill found it very hard work.
"Phew!" he said at the top. "I didn't think we'd make it!"
"Neither did I," replied Ben. "It's a good thing I kept the brake on or we'd have slid back down the hill."

OLLIE: Let's have a race to say the alphabet.
DOLLY: OK.
OLLIE: The alphabet. I beat you!

CANDY STORE

BILLY: What's the quickest way to the candy store?
MILLY: Running!

JIM: Think of the numbers three, five, seven and eleven.
TIM: OK. I'm thinking.
JIM: Now close your eyes.
TIM: Right.
JIM: Dark, isn't it?

HIL: How's your new guitar?
WILL: I threw it away.
HIL: Why?
WILL: It had a hole in the middle of it.

"Even when my pockets are empty I still have something in them."
"What's that?"
"Holes!"

"Old candy wrappers, empty cans, banana skins, soggy tea-bags ..."
"What are you doing?"
"Talking garbage!"

One break time, Cynthia insisted on singing. After she'd sung six songs she turned round and, beaming, said to her friends, "What shall I sing next?"
"Do you know Loch Lomond," asked one.
"Yes," she replied.
"Then go and jump in it!"

What kind of song do you sing in a car?
A car-toon!

TRACEY: I've got cheese with holes in my sandwiches. I don't like cheese with holes in.
STACEY: Then eat the cheese and leave the holes at the side of your plate.

GEMMA: I've got tuna sandwiches again. Every day I get tuna sandwiches, and I hate them!
EMMA: Why don't you tell your mother you don't like them?
GEMMA: Why tell her? She doesn't make my sandwiches, I do!

Bertie was searching the playground for something.
"What are you looking for?" asked Freddie.
"A frog," replied Bertie.
"What do you want a frog for?" asked Freddie.
"To put in my sister's bed," answered Bertie.

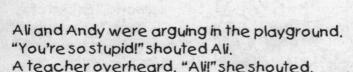

"Why do you want to put a frog in her bed?" persisted Freddie.
"Because I couldn't find a mouse," answered Bertie.

Ali and Andy were arguing in the playground.
"You're so stupid!" shouted Ali.
A teacher overheard. "Ali!" she shouted.
"You mustn't say that! Now say you're sorry!"
"OK," said Ali. "I'm sorry you're stupid, Andy."

PATTIE: One of my ancestors died at Waterloo.
HATTIE: Really?
PATTIE: Yes, he fell under a train at platform seven.

SHELLEY: Do you think I'm vain?
KELLY: No, why do you ask?
SHELLEY: Because most girls as pretty as me usually are.

How do you start a teddy-bear race?
Say, "Ready, teddy, go!"

DONNIE: Have you heard the joke about the peacock?
RONNIE: No.
DONNIE: It's a beautiful tail.

What can you put in your left hand but not your right hand? Your right elbow.

What can you give someone but still keep? Your word.

What turns without moving? Milk, when it goes sour.

What's the hottest letter of the alphabet? B. It makes oil boil.

What's got a bottom at its top?
A leg.

Why did the loony throw
his watch out of the
window?
To see time fly.

What runs but has no legs?
A tap.

What walks around on its head all day?
A nail in your shoe.

KEN: My sister's going to marry an Irishman.
LEN: Oh, really?
KEN: No, O'Reilly.

TIM: Last week my sister took the first step toward getting divorced.
JIM: Did she go to see a solicitor?
TIM: No. She got married.

GILLIE: I got twenty valentine cards this year.
TILLY: Gosh! I've never had that many!
GILLIE: Trouble was, by the time I'd paid for them all I couldn't afford to post them.

MICK: Why have you got a sausage stuck behind your ear?
DICK: What? Oh dear, I must have eaten my pencil at lunchtime.

MOLLY: A can of Coke, please.
SHOPKEEPER: How would you like a free one?
MOLLY: I'd love one, but how come?
SHOPKEEPER: We're giving them away free with every $1 bag of crisps.

JOHN: You've got your cap on back to front.
DON: How do you know which way I'm going?

JANE: Are you trying to make a fool out of me?
WAYNE: No, I never interfere with nature.

JULIE: When I grow up I'm going to marry the boy next door.
JENNY: Why's that?
JULIE: I'm not allowed to cross the road.

ANDY: We've lost our dog.
MANDY: Why don't you put an advert in the paper?
ANDY: Because he can't read.

Laurie was stopped by a police officer for riding his bicycle at a furious speed.
"Why are you going so fast, lad?" he asked.
"Because," replied Laurie, "my brakes don't work very well and I wanted to get home before I had an accident."

DAVE: What did your father say when your brother was sent to jail?
MAVE: "Hello, son."

Why did Sally stand on her head in the playground?
She was turning things over in her mind.

Why did Annie take her bicycle to school?
Because she wanted to drive her teacher up the wall.

RYAN: Do you know anyone who's been on TV?
BRIAN: My little brother did once but he's potty-trained now.

Knock, knock.
Who's there?
Ahab.
Ahab who?
Ahab to go to the bathroom in a hurry, open the door!

What is it that men do standing up, ladies do sitting down and dogs do on three legs?
Shake hands.

When is a white dog not a white dog?
When it's a greyhound.

GERRY: My dog's got no nose.
KERRY: How does he smell?
GERRY: Terrible!

GINNY: Have you heard the joke about the butter?
WINNIE: No, what is it?
GINNY: I'd better not tell you, you might spread it around!

What do you call a cat who's swallowed a duck?
A duck-filled fatty-puss.

What cat is useful in
a library?
A catalog.

Where can a pupil in
the playground find
diamonds?
In a pack of cards.

Table
Manners

If you stay to school dinners, better push them aside, A lot of kids didn't, a lot of kids died.

Why are school cooks cruel?
Because they batter fish, beat eggs and whip cream.

What's the difference between school semolina and frogspawn?
Not a lot!

JENNY: I hear it's UFOs for dinner again.
KENNY: What are UFOs?
JENNY: Unidentified Frying Objects.

TED: Why do you call this
Enthusiasm Curry?
NED: Because the cook's put
everything she's got into it.

Where's the best place in school to have the
sickroom?
Next to the canteen!

SALLY (inspecting her plate): These beans look
old and shrivelled.
SANDRA: Yes, they're not beans, they're has-
beens.

Why are school
sausages so noisy?
Because they're
bangers.

Why are school
sausages so rude?
Because they spit in the
frying pan.

FUSSY FLORA: Excuse me, but this egg
tastes peculiar.
DINNER LADY: Don't blame me, I only
laid the table.

What's the best food to go with a
jacket potato?
Button mushrooms.

95

JEZ: This food isn't fit for a pig to eat!
JOSH: I'll see if they've got any that is.

Will and Gill were comparing school meals with their mothers' cooking.
"My mum's not that good a cook," said Gill, "but at least her gravy moves about on the plate."

JIM: That dinner lady had her thumb in my gravy!
TIM: Don't worry, it's not hot.

What did the hamburger say to the relish?
"That's enough of your sauce!"

DINAH: Excuse me, Miss, are slugs good to eat?
TEACHER: Don't be disgusting, Dinah. Eat up your dinner and I'll speak to you later.
TEACHER (later): Now, Dinah, what was it you wanted to know?
DINAH: I asked if slugs were good to eat, Miss, because you had one on your plate but it's all right, it's gone now.

What's worse than finding a worm in your apple?
Finding half a worm!

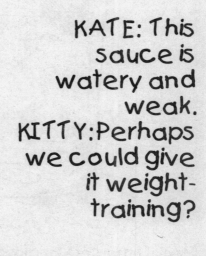

KATE: This sauce is watery and weak.
KITTY: Perhaps we could give it weight-training?

What was the fly doing on the ice cream?
Learning to ski.

DENNIS: Gosh, that pie crust was tough!
DENISE: Pie crust? You've just eaten
your plate!

LIZZIE: My plate's all wet.
LIZA: I expect that's your soup.

JANE: This water's all cloudy.
SHANE (inspecting glass): No it isn't, it's just the
glass that's dirty.

ANNE: There's not much chicken in this chicken
pie.
ALAN: I don't expect there were any shepherds in
the shepherd's pie, either.

What was the fly doing in the soup?
It had committed insecticide.

HARRY: I'm sorry I spilled water on you.
BARRY: That's all right, my jumper was too big anyway.

BEN: My apple pie tastes of soap.
LEN: I expect that's to wash it down with.

What can a whole apple
do that half an apple
can't?
Look
round.

How do you make an apple turnover?
Give it a push.

How do you make an apple puff?
Chase it round the garden.

How do you make a Swiss roll?
Push him off an Alp.

Simon and Sammy
were talking about
the sandwiches
they'd got in their
lunch boxes.
"Mine are tongue,"
said Simon.
"Ugh!" said Sammy.
"Fancy eating
something that's
come out of an
animal's mouth!"
"What have you got,
then?" asked Simon.
"Egg," replied
Sammy.

What happens if you wrap your sandwiches in a comic?
You get crumby jokes.

What kind of cake would most schoolchildren not mind going without?
A cake of soap.

How can you make cakes light?
Make them with petrol and decorate them with matches.

Why didn't the school canteen serve elephant sandwiches?
They didn't have enough bread.

What swings from cake to cake and tastes of almonds?
Tarzipan.

Why did daft Derek mop up his milk with his cake?
It was a sponge cake.

Which cake ruled half the world?
Attila the Bun.

What kind of cake did the school chaplain like?
Angel cake.

What did the toaster say to the bread?
"Pop up and see me sometime."

What do French children eat for breakfast?
Huit heures bix.

What did the slice of toast say to the margarine?
"I'm old enough to know butter."

An accident happened to my brother Jim
When somebody threw a tomato at him.
Tomatoes are squashy, and don't hurt the skin,
But this one was specially packed in a tin.

Did you hear the joke about the potatoes?
They didn't see eye to eye.

Why did the farmer plant razor blades next to his potatoes?
He wanted to grow chips.

Where
were potatoes
first found?
In the ground.

Which Middle Eastern gentleman invented flavored crisps?
Sultan Vinegar.

What are round, green and smell fishy?
Brussels sprats.

What do you call two rows of cabbages?
A dual cabbageway.

What's the difference between a fish and a violin?
You can't tune a fish.

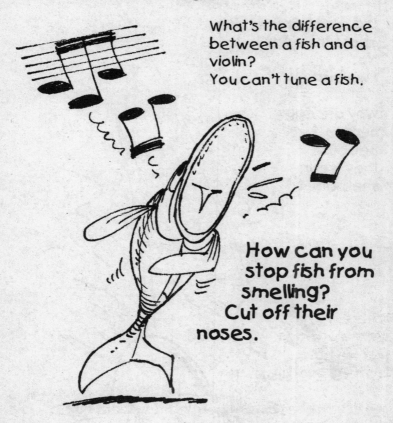

How can you stop fish from smelling?
Cut off their noses.

What goes up brown or white and
comes down yellow and white?
An egg.

What do you call a mischievous
egg?
A practical yolker.

Did you hear the joke
about the eggs?
No.
Two bad.

Why are eggs
nerds?
Because
they wear
shellsuits.

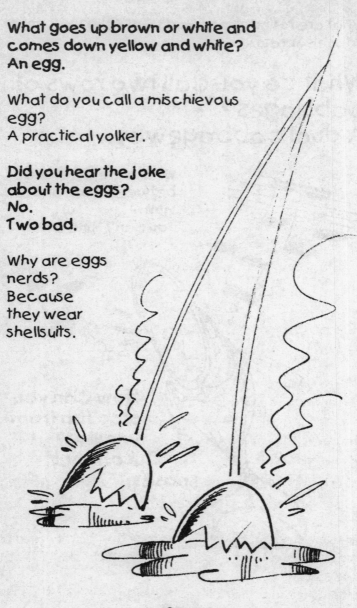

How do you get a hen to lay hard-boiled eggs?
Put her in a hot bath.

What's yellow and brown and hairy?
Cheese on toast dropped on the carpet.

Did you hear about the two-handed cheese?
You eat it with one hand and hold your nose with the other.

The class was having its photograph taken, and to make them all smile the teacher said, "Say 'cheese.'"
"Gor-gon-zola," said naughty Nigel.

If cheese comes after pudding, what comes after cheese?
Mice.

What stays hot in the fridge?
A hamburger with too much mustard on it.

How do you make a Mexican chilli?
Take him to Alaska.

What has one horn and gives milk?
A milk lorry.

When is it OK to serve milk in a saucer?
When you give it to a cat.

How does a coffee pot feel when it's full?
Perky.

What kind of food is Chinese
and deadly?
Chop sueycide.

Jonathan
was sprawling at
his desk with his feet
stuck out where
people would fall over
them, and chewing gum.
His teacher spotted him,
and called out angrily,
"Jonathan, take that gum
out of your mouth and put
your feet in this instant!"

Why did Darren put his father in the freezer?
He wanted ice-cold pop.

What's a frog's favorite drink?
Croaka-cola.

Two of the senior girls stopped at a teashop on the way home and ordered tea and buns. The first took a sip of her tea and said, "Ugh! This is disgusting! It tastes like gasoline!"
The second sipped hers and agreed. They called the waitress. "Is this meant to be tea or coffee?" asked the first girl. "It tastes like gasoline!"
"In that case it's tea," said the waitress. "The coffee tastes like paraffin."

"Will you join me in a cup of tea?" the art teacher asked the science teacher.
"Do you think there'd be room for both of us?" the science teacher replied.

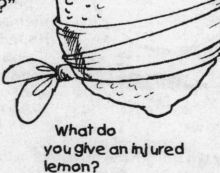

What do you give an injured lemon?
Lemon-aid.

How do you make gold soup?
Put fourteen carrots in it.

How long do the Italians eat spaghetti?
About 30 cm.

Annie, Bertie and Chris went into the candy store on their way home from school. Annie asked for a nickel's worth of aniseed balls.
The jar containing the aniseed balls was on the top shelf, so the shopkeeper went to the room behind the shop, brought back a stepladder and climbed up to get the jar. When she'd measured out the aniseed balls and taken Annie's money, she replaced the jar and took the stepladder back.
"And what would you like?" she asked Bertie.
"I'd like a nickel's worth of aniseed balls too, please," replied Bertie. So the shopkeeper returned to the room behind the shop to get the stepladder, climbed up, got the jar again and measured out the aniseed balls.
When she'd done so, she looked at Chris. "I suppose you'd like a nickel's worth of aniseed balls too, would you?" she asked.
"No thank you," he replied. So the shopkeeper replaced the jar on the top shelf and took the stepladder back again.
When she returned she asked Chris what he would like.
"I'd like a dime's worth of aniseed balls, please," he replied.

Why aren't bananas
ever lonely?
They hang around in
bunches.

What's yellow and writes?
A ballpoint banana.

How do you make a banana split?
Slice it in half.

What does a grape say when you tread on it?
Nothing, it just lets out a little wine.

TEACHER: Please don't eat off your knife, Betty,
use a fork.
BETTY: But, Miss, my fork leaks.

I eat my peas with honey,
I've done it all my life.
It makes the peas taste funny, but
It keeps them on the knife!

How many peas in a pint?
Only one!

What's the best food for would-be athletes?
Runner beans.

What do you get if you cross a tin of baked beans
with a birthday cake?
A cake that blows out its own candles.

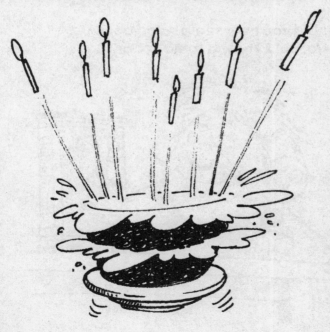

The geography teacher had been a bit of an explorer in his youth.

"Once," he told the class, "when I was shipwrecked, I lived on a tin of baked beans for a week."

"Please, Sir," interrupted a small boy, "weren't you afraid of falling off?"

What two things should you never eat before breakfast?
Lunch and tea.

What do religious vegetarians say before dinner?
"Lettuce pray."

JOHN: Did you ever see a salad bowl?
RON: No, but I know a tomato can.

On the Sick List

WAYNE (speaking on phone): I'm afraid Wayne has a cold and can't come to school today.
TEACHER: To whom am I speaking?
WAYNE: This is my father.

What can you keep and give away at the same time?
A cold.

Why can you run faster when you've got a cold?
Because you have a racing pulse and a running nose.

TEACHER: Is your cough better, Brian?
BRIAN: It should be, I've been practicing all night.

Why did Jim's grandpa put his hand to his mouth when he sneezed?
To catch his teeth.

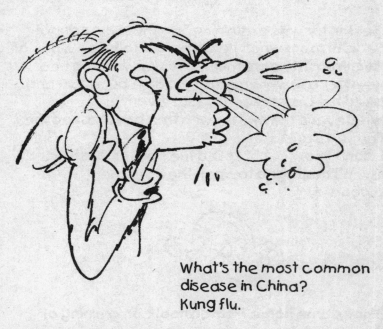

What's the most common disease in China?
Kung flu.

When does a flu virus think it's successful?
When it brings someone to their sneeze.

The school doctor was examining Nigel.
"Take a deep breath," he said, "then breathe out three times."
"Do you want to check my lungs?" asked Nigel.
"No," replied the doctor, "I want to clean my glasses."

Why was trendy Tina offended when the doctor examined her?
He told her she'd got acute appendicitis.

"Just let me take your pulse," said the school nurse.
"Haven't you got one of your own?" asked Derek.

The doctor was examining Sammy in the school medical room when he came out to fetch a pair of pliers from the caretaker who was working near by. After a few moments he came out again and asked the caretaker for a screwdriver.
"Whatever's the matter with that boy?" asked the alarmed caretaker.
"I don't know yet," replied the doctor. "I still haven't managed to open the instrument cupboard."

Ginny came home from school complaining of stomach ache.
"I expect it's because your stomach's empty and you're hungry," said her Mom. "If you put something in it you'll feel better."
Later Ginny's dad came home from work complaining of a headache. "I expect it's because your head's empty," said Ginny. "Put something in it and you'll feel better."

What's the matter with you if your nose runs and your feet smell? You're built upside down.

SCHOOL DOCTOR: How's your broken rib, Archie?
ARCHIE: I keep getting a stitch in my side, Doctor.
SCHOOL DOCTOR: Good. That shows the bone is knitting.

"Doctor, can you cure my spots?"
"I never make rash promises."

Susie had a sore throat and the doctor told her to go over to the window and stick out her tongue.
"Will you be able to see it better over there?" she asked.
"No," admitted the doctor. "It's just that I don't like the people across the road."

Mrs Brown took her son Tom to the doctor.
"He keeps pulling horrible faces," she said.
"That doesn't sound much to worry about," replied
the doctor.
"It is to the horrible faces, though," retorted Mrs
Brown.

"Did you learn anything new in school today, son?"
asked Ben's dad.
"Only how to get out of math by painting red spots
on my face," answered Ben.

Laura had been off school for a week.
"How do you feel today?" asked her mom.
"Same as always, with my hands," answered Laura.

DENNIS: How did
you manage to
break your
ankle?
DAVE: See those
steps outside the
gymnasium?
DENNIS: Yes.
DAVE: I didn't.

It was exam time and Fenton was having trouble sleeping.
"Do what I do," said his dad, "count sheep."
"I tried that," said Fenton, "but by the time I'd got to 8,475, it was time to get up."

MO: My brother's off school because my sister broke an arm.
JOE: Why is your brother off if your sister broke an arm?
MO: It was his arm she broke!

The class were having their eyesight checked. Molly walked in and said, "Do you think I need glasses, Doctor?"
"I think you might, Molly," a voice replied. "I'm your principal."

OPTICIAN: Have you ever had your eyes checked?
DOTTY: No, they've always been brown.

OPTICIAN: You need glasses.
KATE: But I'm already wearing glasses.
OPTICIAN: Then I need glasses.

MICK: Why do you need three pairs of glasses?
NICK: One for distance; one for reading; and one to help me find the other two.

How can you tell when your teacher has a glass eye? When it comes out in conversation.

Jen's grandad was very deaf and the family was pleased when he got a new hearing aid. "Can you hear me now, Grandpa?" asked Jen. "Last Thursday," replied Grandpa.

What did one ear say to the other?
"I didn't know we lived on the same block."

What's the right time to go to the dentist?
Two-thirty (tooth-hurty).

TEACHER: Why weren't you at school yesterday?
JIMMY: I had a bad tooth, Sir.
TEACHER: Oh dear. Is it better now?
JIMMY: I don't know, I left it at the dentist.

What did one tooth say to the other?
"There's gold in them there fills."

JOSIE: You said the dentist would be painless but he wasn't.
MUM: Did he hurt you?
JOSIE: No, but he screamed when I bit his finger.

JOHNNY: Mom says I must make an appointment to see the dentist.
RECEPTIONIST: I'm afraid he's away at present.
JOHNNY: Oh good. When do you expect him to be away again?

Why are dentists artistic?
They spend their time
drawing teeth.

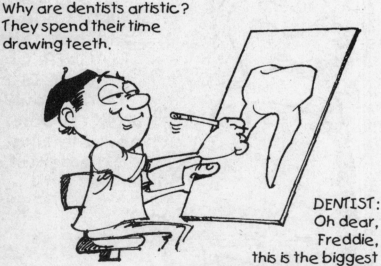

DENTIST: Oh dear, Freddie, this is the biggest cavity I've ever seen, biggest cavity I've ever seen, biggest cavity I've ever seen ...
FREDDIE: You don't need to keep on saying so.
DENTIST: I didn't. That was an echo.

DENTIST: There's no need to pull such a face, Samantha, I haven't even touched your teeth yet.
SAMANTHA: I know. But you're standing on my foot.

TEACHER: Why are you crying, Ella?
ELLA (sniffing): Because Bella said I was deaf and dumb.
BELLA: I never said you were deaf!

Why did the nurse write on Benny's toes?
He was just adding a footnote.

MRS TUBBY: I think Terry's a bit run down.
DOCTOR: Tell him to look both ways before he crosses the road.

After playing rugby all afternoon, Craig complained that every bone in his body hurt. "Be thankful you're not a herring," said his games teacher.

How did daft Derek get a splinter in his finger? He scratched his head.

What do you call a nurse with greasy fingers?
A medicine dropper.

ANDY: I keep seeing double.
DOCTOR: Lie down on the couch, please.
ANDY: The one on the right or the one on the left?

What happened when the principal was sent to hospital? He took a turn for the nurse.

GILLY: The doctor told me to take two pills on an empty stomach.
BILLY: Did they make you better?
GILLY: Not really — they kept rolling off in the night.

DOCTOR: Take one of these pills three times a day.
CLEVER CLARENCE: How can I take it more than once?

DOCTOR: What can I do for you, Micky?
MICKY: It's my brother, Doctor. He thinks he's an elevator.
DOCTOR: Tell him to come in.
MICKY: I can't. He doesn't stop at this floor.

BERTIE: My mom asked the doctor for something for wind.
GERTIE: What did he do?
BERTIE: He gave her a kite.

What does the doctor do if he finds you have flat feet? Gives you a bicycle pump.

BERYL: I think there's something wrong with my stomach.
DOCTOR: Well, keep your coat buttoned up and no one will notice.

CHERYL: I snore so loudly I keep myself awake. What should I do?
DOCTOR: Sleep in another room.

Sheila broke her wrist and had her arm and hand in a plaster cast.
"When you take it off," she asked the doctor, "will I be able to play the piano?"
"Yes, of course," he replied.
"That's odd, I never could before," said Sheila.

MOTHER: It's time for your medicine.
SHAUN: I'll turn on the bath, shall I?
MOTHER: Whatever for?
SHAUN: The label on the bottle says "To be taken in water."

TEACHER: Why were you absent yesterday, Craig?
CRAIG: My hearing was bad, Miss.
TEACHER: You mean you had earache?
CRAIG: No, I didn't hear the alarm clock.

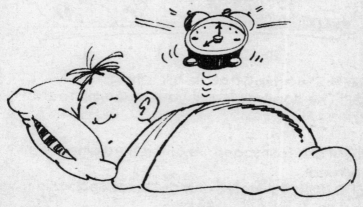

Young Sarah was overweight and confessed to the nurse that she was worried about her figure. "You'll have to diet," said the nurse. "Do you think so?" asked Sarah. "What color?"

Jimmy managed to cut himself badly doing woodwork and was rushed off to hospital. "I'll have to put some stitches in," said the doctor. "While you're doing it," said Jimmy, "do you think you could mend this tear in my trousers?"

NOREEN: I'm having trouble breathing.
NURSE: The doctor will give you something to stop that.

NURSE: Take four spoonfuls of this medicine after every meal.
DAFT DEREK: But we've only got three spoons in our house.

MILLY: I've swallowed a mouth organ!
DOCTOR: Be thankful you don't play the piano.

TILLY: I keep thinking I'm invisible.
DOCTOR: Next!

How do you cure water on the brain?
With a tap on the head.

What should you do if you swallow a spoon? Lie down and don't stir.

What should you do if you can't sleep?
Lie on the edge of the bed —
you'll soon drop off.

TEDDY: My brother thinks he's a bridge.
DOCTOR: What's come over him?

Why did the school doctor
give up his job?
He didn't have the patients.

WALLY: I feel like a yo-yo.
DOCTOR: Sit down, stand up, sit down.

SALLY: I feel like a violin.
DOCTOR: Sit down while I make some notes.

DOCTOR: There's nothing wrong with you, you're just lazy.
ANDY: Can you tell me the medical name for that so I can tell my teacher?

MANDY: My sister thinks she's a dog.
DOCTOR: Have you felt her nose?

MRS SMITH: I'm afraid little Samantha keeps stealing things.
DOCTOR: These pills should help.
MRS SMITH: But what if they don't?
DOCTOR: Ask her to pick me up a video camera.

What happens if you think you're a strawberry?
You're in a jam!

What happens if you think you're a dumpling?
You're in a stew!

What happens if you think
you're an onion?
You're in a pickle!

What happens if you think you're shrinking?
You'll have to be a little patient!

SCHOOL NURSE: Don't worry, the new doctor's very funny, he'll have you in stitches!
NERVOUS NORA: I hope not, I'm only here to have a flu jab.

KATIE: What's the new school doctor like?
CATHY: Great! He's so sympathetic he really makes you feel ill.

When Wally asked the doctor how he stood, the doctor replied that he'd no idea. He reckoned it was a miracle.

SCHOOL DOCTOR: How do you feel, Samantha?
SAMANTHA: Much better, thank you, Doctor, I feel like my old self again.
SCHOOL DOCTOR: In that case you need more treatment.

TICK TOCK!

TICK TOCK!

LESLEY: I think my
little brother's
swallowed a clock!
WESLEY: How alarming!

What should you do if you feel
like a pair of curtains?
Pull yourself together.

School
Treats

A group of children from a school in the city center went for a country ramble and found a crate full of empty milk bottles at the side of a lane. "Come quickly!" shouted one little boy, "I've found a cow's nest!"

The school once went on an outing by train to the seaside, and the journey hadn't been progressing for very long when the teacher rushed up to the conductor and said, "Stop the train! Stop the train! One of the children has just fallen off!"
"That's all right," he replied calmly. "They'd all paid for their tickets."

On another occasion the class was booked on a ferry and the principal was going through the safety drill. "What would you do," she asked, "if one of the children fell overboard?"
"Shout 'Pupil overboard,'" replied a boy.
"Good," said the principal. "And what if one of the teachers fell overboard?"
"Er, which one?" asked a cautious girl.

"Did you enjoy the school outing?" asked Mother.
"Oh, yes," said Jemima. "And we're going again tomorrow."
"Really?" asked Mother. "Whatever for?"
"To look for the children who got left behind."

DOLLY: We're doing a school play.
POLLY: *Hamlet?*
DOLLY: No, more like *Piglet.*

MOLLY: Does your school play
have a happy ending?
POLLY: I'll say! I was very happy
when it had ended!

PETER: Every Wednesday afternoon our teacher
takes us out and we go for a tramp in the woods.
ANITA: That sounds nice. Does the class enjoy it?
PETER: Yes, but the tramp's getting a bit fed up.

The class was on a field study trip in the
countryside.
"What a pretty cow that is," said Annie.
"That's a Jersey," said her teacher.
"Really?" asked Annie. "I thought it was her skin."

LEN: Where did you go on your school trip?
KEN: We flew to Paris.
LEN: Didn't it make your arms tired?

What's tall, good to eat and stands in the middle of Paris?
The Trifle Tower.

When the class went on a trip to the seaside, they stayed at a small hotel that advertised "Bed and Board." The trouble was, they said afterwards, it was difficult to know which was the bed and which was the board.

Mrs Twigg took her class on a nature ramble. They went past a large duck pond.
"Be careful not to fall in, children," she said, "the water's very deep."
"But it can't be, Miss," said Susie, "it only comes up to the middle of those ducks."

RILEY: How did you find the weather on your school trip?
KYLIE: I just walked outside and there it was.

Lady Widebehind was giving the school a talk about her travels in the East.
"Remember, children," she told them, "travel broadens the mind."
"If you're anything to go by, that's not all it broadens," muttered Gill to Phil.

What did the school wit say as the class boarded the boat?
"Every time I go on a ferry it makes me cross."

DEIRDRE: I wish we could go somewhere really wild and remote on our school trip.
DORA: Why?
DEIRDRE: I want to go where the hand of man has never set foot.

One year the school went to the Natural History Museum in London.
"Did you enjoy it?" asked a teacher on the way home.
"Oh yes," replied the class. "But it was a bit funny going to a dead zoo."

How did the school bus get a puncture?
Because of the fork in the road.

When the class went on a trip at Easter, Milly and Molly disappeared. Milly was very tall and Molly was very short. The teachers hunted high and low for them.

When Maureen also disappeared after the school trip, her teacher asked her mother if she'd given a description of the girl to the police.
"I tried," said Maureen's mother, "but they didn't believe me."

Johnnie was boasting that he'd got a part in the school nativity play.
"What part will you play?" asked his friend Donnie.
"I'm one of the three wise guys," replied Johnnie.

How did the two Christmas angels greet each other?
They said, "Halo."

The class were drawing the backdrop to the Christmas play, and their teacher was walking round examining their work. She looked at the manger, the shepherds, the cattle and the sheep, then noticed a square object in the corner.
"What's that?" she asked.
"Oh," replied little Chrissie, "that's their television set."

KELSEY: Why is your school play called a miracle play?
CHELSEA: Because it'll be a miracle if we get it right!

The school had given a concert and Mrs Feather's son had played the piano. She was very proud of him. She asked his music teacher, "Do you think my Freddie should take up the piano as a career?"
"No," replied the music teacher, "I think he should put down the lid as a favor."

Why did they arrest the music teacher?
He got into treble.

JIMMY: Why do you always play the same piece of music at the school concert?
TIMMY: Because it haunts me.
JIMMY: I'm not surprised, you murdered it weeks ago.

SHELLEY: My dad is a very good pianist. He can even play with his feet.
NELLIE: How old is your dad?
SHELLEY: Thirty-five.
NELLIE: Pooh! My little brother can play with his feet and he's only two!

The school went to Paris for Easter and when the holiday was nearly over Sally said to Susie, "We've been here four days and we haven't been to the Louvre yet."
"I know," said Susie. "It must be the change of diet."

When the school went to London, they met a man carrying a violin who asked them the way to the Festival Hall. "Practice!" replied smarty-pants Susie.

While they were in London, they went to the Tate Gallery to look at the modern paintings. A very hoity-toity lady said to the guide, "And I suppose that hideous sight is what you call a work of art!"
"No, madam," he replied, "that's what you call a mirror."

On the train coming home Davy asked the teacher, "What was the name of that station we just stopped at?"
"I didn't notice," replied the teacher. "I was reading. Why do you ask?"
"I thought you'd like to know where Eddie and Freddie got off."

Paddy was very nervous about going in a plane. "Do these planes crash often?" he asked the stewardess.
"No," she smiled, "only once."

BOOM! BOOM!!

What's yellow and white and travels faster than sound? An egg sandwich on Concorde.

What happens when a plane runs out of fuel?
All the passengers get out to push.

PASSENGER: Does this plane fly faster than sound?
STEWARDESS: No, sir.
PASSENGER: That's good because my friend and I have lots to talk about.

Why is a plane like a con man?
Neither has any visible means of support.

Where in America would those members of the
class who enjoyed dancing like to visit?
San Frandisco.

Which American city would a cow like to visit?
Moo York.

When little Jimmy went to America he made
friends with young Hank. Trying to impress him,
Jimmy said, "My great-great grandfather was
touched on the shoulder with a sword by
Queen Victoria and that made him a knight."
"Gee, that's nothing," said Hank. "My great-
great-grandfather was touched on the head
with a tomahawk by a Cheyenne Indian and
that made him an angel!"

Johnny was asked if he could spell "Mississippi." He replied, "Well, I can start, but I'm not sure when to stop."

What do you call an American drawing?
A Yankee doodle.

TEDDY: If you were walking through a Canadian forest and you met a bear, would you keep on walking or turn round and run?
EDDIE: I'd turn round and run.
TEDDY: What, with a bear behind?

BONNIE: I'm so glad I wasn't born in Germany.
DONNY: Why?
BONNIE: I can't speak any German!

The class was taken to visit the opera, and afterwards young Daniel was asked if he had enjoyed it.
"Oh, yes," he replied. "But why did that man with a stick keep hitting that lady?"
"He wasn't hitting her, he was conducting the orchestra," said his teacher.
"But if he wasn't hitting her, why was she screaming?" asked Daniel.

BARBARA: Do you like opera?
BRENDA: Apart from the singing, yes.

When 2B was taken to a concert, Sally asked why the members of the orchestra kept looking at their books.
"That's the score," explained the music teacher.
"Really?" said Sally. "Who won?"

PRINCIPAL: How's the new school bus driver coming along?
VICE PRINCIPAL: He's trying.
PRINCIPAL: I've heard he's very trying!

PASSENGER: Does this bus go to London?
BUS DRIVER: No.
PASSENGER: But it says "London" on the front.
BUS DRIVER: It says "Fish fingers" on the side but we don't sell them!

What's red and lies upside down in the gutter?
A dead London bus.

TEACHER: Did you say you fell over 60 feet and didn't hurt yourself?
DONALD: Yes, I was trying to get off the school bus.

"Does this bus stop at the seafront?"
"If it doesn't there'll be an awfully big splash!"

What's the difference between a bus driver and a cold?
One knows the stops; the other stops the nose.

Knock, knock.
Who's there?
Venice.
Venice who?
Venice the next plane to Italy?

What do you call false Italian spaghetti?
Mockoroni.

Which Italian secret society beats people up with shopping baskets?
The Raffia.

What can you see from
the top of the Eiffel
Tower?
Quite an eyeful!

What do you call a
nervous Middle Eastern
gentleman?
The Shake of Araby.

What did one Egyptian say to another?
"I don't remember your name but your fez is
familiar."

What's the best thing about going on a school trip?
Coming home!

Testing Times

DAD: Did you get a good place in your exams, son?
SON: Oh, yes, Dad, I sat next to the school swot.

TEACHER: I hope I didn't see you cheating, Aggie.
AGGIE: I hope you didn't, too, Miss.

HARRY: I've just saved you $10, Dad.
DAD: How come?
HARRY: You remember you said you'd give me $10 if I passed my exams?
DAD: Yes.
HARRY: Well, I didn't.

DAD: You did very badly in your exams, Darren, bottom out of thirty!
DARREN: It could have been worse, Dad.
DAD: How?
DARREN: If I'd been in a bigger class I might have been bottom out of fifty!

TEACHER: Your handwriting's terrible, Tina.
TINA: I know, Miss, but if it was better you'd realize
I couldn't spell!

Which animals are good at exams?
Cheetahs.

What exams does Santa
Claus take?
Ho, ho, ho levels.

Did you hear about the
teacher who did bird
impressions when the
class were sitting their
exams?
She watched them
like a hawk.

What does a teacher
have that her class
doesn't?
The answers.

MOTHER: Why are you spanking Freddie?
FATHER: Because his exam results are due out tomorrow and I'll be away on business all day.

How do dinosaurs pass exams?
With extinction.

Knock, knock.
Who's there?
Gladys.
Gladys who?
Gladys the end of exams!

One question in Sarah's biology exam asked the difference between an African elephant and an Indian elephant. Sarah wrote, "About 5,000 kilometers."

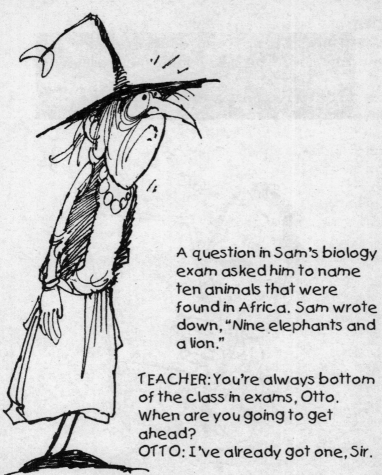

A question in Sam's biology exam asked him to name ten animals that were found in Africa. Sam wrote down, "Nine elephants and a lion."

TEACHER: You're always bottom of the class in exams, Otto. When are you going to get ahead?
OTTO: I've already got one, Sir.

OLIVER: I didn't think I deserved a nought for my math exam.
MATH TEACHER: Neither did I, but we don't give minus marks.

Why did the student witch fail her exams?
She was so bad at spelling.

TEACHER: Why do you always fail your exams, Sam?
SAM: Because you always set the wrong questions, Sir.

Sam's class has a history of producing magnificent mistakes in their exam papers.
Here are some of the most notable ones.

Margarine is butter made from imitation cows.

Jacob's brother was called See-Saw.

Jesus walked down the road with the rabbits.

King Henry VIII had an abbess on his knee which made it difficult for him to walk.

King Henry VIII disillusioned the monasteries.

A plumber is someone who picks plums.

King Henry
VIII's second
wife was
called Anne
Berlin.

A centurion was a Roman
soldier who was 100 years old.

A fjord is a Norwegian motor car.

People who live in Paris are called Parasites.

The Equator is an
imaginary lion running
right round the earth.

Mercury was a Greek god who
can now be found in a
thermometer.

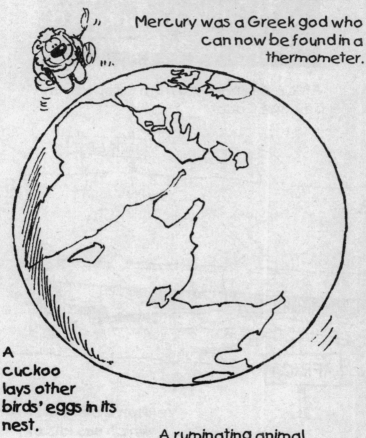

A
cuckoo
lays other
birds' eggs in its
nest.

A ruminating animal
chews its cubs.

Sir Francis Drake made the Armada wait while he finished his game of bowels.

Africa is separated from Europe by the Sewage Canal.

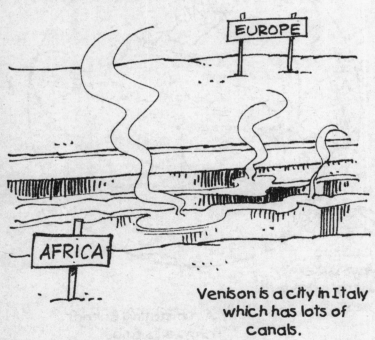

Venison is a city in Italy which has lots of canals.

Insects is something burned in churches.

Tadpoles eat one another until they become frogs.

Hot air rises by conviction.

An optimist is someone who tests people's eyes.

Conservation is when you talk to people.

Young doctors practice medicine until they get it right

An allegory is when something makes you sneeze, like hay fever.

Cleopatra died from the bite of a wasp.

The kidneys are infernal organs.

164

The Roman LXX stands for "love and kisses."

My auntie's in the Middle Ages.

An insect with 100 legs is called a centimeter.

The horizon is where the land meets the sky but it isn't there when you get there.

165

Joan of Ark was Noah's wife.

A curve is the longest line between two points.

A woman whose husband has died is called a window.

Manilla is where envelopes come from.

Shakespeare wrote tragedy, comedy and errors.

Taxes is a state in America which has lots of cowboys.

An oxygen is something that has eight sides.

Trees are sometimes planted to break wind.

The Stock Exchange is where sheep, cattle and pigs are bought and sold.

Which girl is *very* good at exams?
Anne Sirs.

When Angela had to write down on her exam paper the name of a liquid that won't freeze, she wrote "hot water."

DAD: Why have you done so badly in your exams recently? You used to get quite good marks.
JASON: It's the teacher's fault.
DAD: Why do you say that?
JASON: I used to sit next to the cleverest boy in the class but she moved him!

MOM: Did you get a good place in your exams?
JANET: Oh yes, I sat next to the radiator.

Three friends were walking home from school one sunny afternoon. "What shall we do?" asked one. "Let's toss a coin," said another. "If it comes down heads, we'll go and play football, and if it comes down tails we'll go for a swim in the river." "Good idea," said a third. "And if it lands on its edge we'll go home and study for our exams."

A father took his son to an interview at a private school.
"Do you get good exam results?" he asked.
"Oh yes," replied the principal. "We guarantee it — or we return the boy."

VISITOR: How are you, Hector?
HECTOR: I'm very well, thank you. But I've just had diarrhea, pneumonia, eczema and varicose veins.
VISITOR: Oh dear! How terrible to have all those things at your age!
HECTOR: It was. It was the hardest spelling test I've ever done.

AUNTIE: How were your exam questions?
ANNIE: They were OK. It was the answers I had trouble with.

Lizzie was sitting her French oral exam.
"What does *moi aussi* mean?" asked the examiner.
"Er — I am an Australian?" answered Lizzie.

In the woodwork practical, Serge was asked what was the safest way to use a hammer. "Get someone else to hold the nails," he replied.

Gillie was taking a music exam.
"If 'f' means *forte*, what do you think 'ff' means?" asked her teacher.
"Eighty?" replied Gillie.

Why did daft Dinah stand on a ladder when she took a singing exam?
So she could reach the high notes.

Chamber of Horrors

When Annie first went to school she was puzzled by people talking about the Chamber of Horrors. "What do you mean?" she asked nervously.
"It's what we call the staff room," explained her friend.

What's the difference between a schoolteacher and a monster?
Not a lot!

What's the difference between a schoolteacher and a train?
One says "spit out that sweet"; the other says, "choo, choo"!

MOM: Why don't you like your teacher?
CATHY: Because she told me to sit at the front for the present, but she never gave me the present!

What problem did the cross-eyed teacher have?
She couldn't control her pupils.

What makes teachers special?
Being in a class of their own.

PRINCIPAL: Well, Miss Brown, in the few weeks you've been here you've certainly got this class under control. How do you keep on your toes like this?
NEW YOUNG TEACHER: Every time I sit down they put thumbtacks on my chair.

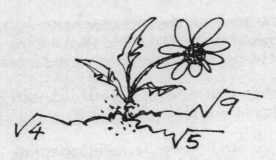

Did you hear what happened when the math teacher brought a plant to school?
It grew square roots.

The chemistry teacher was explaining how acids worked. He held up a beaker of acid and a dime.
"Now," he said, "I'm going to drop the coin into the acid. Do you think the acid will dissolve it?"
"No," said bright Bertie.
"Correct," said the teacher. "But how did you know?"
"Because you wouldn't have dropped the dime in it if it was going to dissolve!" answered Bertie.

The English teacher asked the class to write an essay on what they would do if they won $1 million on the lottery. When the class handed in their papers, Keith's was blank.
"I asked you to write down what you'd do if you won $1 million," said the teacher. "But you have written nothing. Why?"
"Because that's what I'd do," answered Keith.

What was the art teacher happiest to draw?
Her wages.

The new music teacher asked her class if they had managed to pick up music yet.
"Oh, yes," answered Bill and Ben.
"Good," answered the teacher. "In that case you can move the piano for me."

MATH TEACHER: If I slice two apples, three oranges and four bananas into ten pieces each, what will I have?
MILLY: A fruit salad.

MATH TEACHER: If you had seventy-seven cents in one pocket and eighty-five cents in the other, what would you have?
MIKE: Someone else's trousers.

MATH TEACHER: If you had $3.75 and you asked your mother for another $3.75, how much money would you have?
LEN: $3.75.
MATH TEACHER: You don't know your arithmetic, Len.
LEN: You don't know my mother, Sir.

TEACHER: Who can tell me the name of the first woman in the world? Tilly?
TILLY: Don't know, Miss.
TEACHER: Come now, Tilly, it has something to do with an apple.
TILLY: Oh ... was it Granny Smith?

GEOGRAPHY TEACHER: Where are the Andes?
NIGEL: At the end of the armies.

What do you call a geometry teacher? An angler.

HISTORY TEACHER: Why is your history work so poor, Peter?
PETER: I believe in letting bygones be bygones.

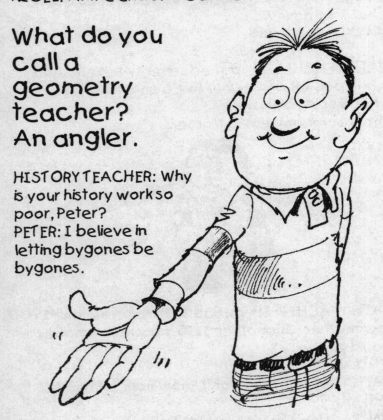

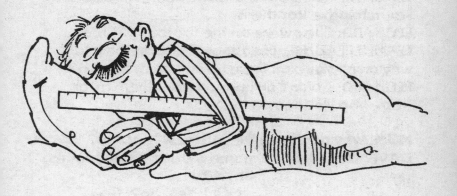

Why did the science teacher take a ruler to bed?
So he could see how long he slept.

CHEMISTRY TEACHER: What does HNO_3 stand for?
PADDY: Er...um...it's on the tip of my tongue.
CHEMISTRY TEACHER: Then you'd better spit it out — it's nitric acid!

HISTORY TEACHER: The Romans conquered France, Italy, Britain — why didn't they continue?
CHARLIE: I expect they ran out of conkers.

GAMES TEACHER: Samantha, you're hopeless at games, gym, and most of your lessons. If you don't try harder you'll never come first in anything!
SAMANTHA: I'm always first in the dinner queue, Sir.

177

GAMES TEACHER: Has anyone seen my glasses? I seem to have lost them.
RICHARD: They were on the football pitch, Sir.
GAMES TEACHER: If you saw them on the pitch why didn't you pick them up and bring them in?
RICHARD: I didn't think you'd want them after Harry had trodden on them, Sir.

MOM: Why don't you like your new teacher?
DAVE: Well, Mom, my name is Dave Mickey Jones, isn't it?

MOM: Yes. So?
DAVE: My teacher just calls me Dave Jones because she says, otherwise, my name's too long.
MOM: Well, what's wrong with that?
DAVE: I don't like having the Mickey taken out of me!

ENGLISH TEACHER: You don't seem to know very much, Angus. Have you read Shakespeare?
ANGUS: No, Sir.
ENGLISH TEACHER: Have you read Dickens?
ANGUS: No, Sir.
ENGLISH TEACHER: Hardy? Jane Austen?
ANGUS: No, Sir.
ENGLISH TEACHER: Well, what *have* you read?
ANGUS: Er, I've red hair, Sir.

NEW TEACHER: Now, class, I want you to give me a list of what we call the lower animals, starting with Jimmy Smith.

TEACHER: Why can you never answer any of my questions?
JENNY: If we could, there wouldn't be much point in being here!

The English teacher was trying to explain what the word "collision" meant. "What would happen," she asked, "if two boys ran into each other in the playground?"
"They'd fight," answered the class.

Neddie was away from school one afternoon, so the next morning his teacher asked him if he'd been off playing football again.
"Certainly not," replied Neddie. "And I've got the jar of tadpoles to prove it."

The bell had signalled the end of break ten minutes before, but Pat was still in the playground. "Pat," called out her teacher, "what are you doing? The bell has gone!"
"Well I didn't take it," answered Pat.

GEOGRAPHY TEACHER: What can you tell me about the Dead Sea?
WILLIAM: I didn't even know it was ill, Sir.

SCIENCE TEACHER: Why don't we fall off the earth?
SIMON: Because of the law of gravity, Sir.
SCIENCE TEACHER: That's right.
SIMON: But what happened to people before the law was passed?

COOKERY TEACHER: Who can tell me the best things to put in a Christmas cake?
SALLY: Your teeth!

TEACHER: Can you spell
the word "needle"?
OLLIE: N, E, I, ...
TEACHER: No, there's no
I in "needle."
OLLIE: Then it's not a very
good needle, is it, Miss?

TEACHER: What is "can't"
short for?
CAROL: "Cannot."
TEACHER: Correct. And what
is "don't" short for?
CAROL: "Doughnut."

TEACHER: Give me a sentence starting with "I."
JOHN: "I is ..."
TEACHER: No, we don't say "I is", we say "I am."
Start again.
JOHN: OK. "I am the ninth letter of the alphabet."

Mr Drear was droning on and on and on one warm
afternoon and the class was getting very bored.
Then the teacher spotted a boy apparently
reading something under his desk.
"Henry!" he roared. "What are you doing? Are you
learning something?"
"Oh no, Sir," replied Henry innocently. "I'm listening
to you."

MATH TEACHER: Suppose, Horace, that your father were to borrow $100 from me and to pay me back at the rate of $5.50 a month. How much would he owe me after six months?

HORACE: $100, Sir.

MATH TEACHER: I'm afraid you don't know much about arithmetic, Horace.

HORACE: And I'm afraid you don't know much about my father, Sir.

MATH TEACHER: What is seven plus three?

OLLIE: Don't know, Sir.

MATH TEACHER: Well, you should. It's ten, of course.

OLLIE: But, Sir, yesterday you said five plus five was ten!

TEACHER: Now, today, we're going to study the wildlife of Africa, starting with elephants. Now pay attention and look at me or you may never know what an elephant looks like!

Why did the teacher wear sunglasses in class?
His pupils were so bright.

TEACHER: Why aren't you writing, Annie?
ANNIE: I ain't got no pencil, Miss.
TEACHER: You mean you have no pencil.
ANNIE: Don't understand, Miss.
TEACHER: I have no pencil, you have no pencil, we have no pencils.
ANNIE: Gosh, Miss, I didn't realize the school was that hard up!

TEACHER: Betty, I told you to write out "I must learn how to spell correctly" fifty times but you've only written it twenty times.
BETTY: I can't count either, Miss.

TEACHER: Can you count up to ten, Angela?
ANGELA: Yes, Miss. One, two, three, four, five, six, seven, eight, nine, ten.
TEACHER: Good. Now what comes after ten?
ANGELA: Jack, queen, king.

TEACHER: Don't shuffle your feet when you walk into assembly. Pick them up.
NAUGHTY NIGEL: When we've picked them up, are we supposed to carry them in our pockets?

ENGLISH TEACHER: This term we're going to study Kipling. Do you like Kipling, Brian?
BRIAN: I don't know, Sir, I've never kippled.

BILL: Our history teacher's hair is beginning to abdicate.
BEN: Abdicate?
BILL: Yes, it's giving up the crown.

Does an apple a day keep a teacher away?
It does if your aim is good enough!

If an apple a day does keep a teacher away, what does an onion a day do?
Keeps everyone away!

Why was Harold kept in a cage in the classroom?
He was the teacher's pet.

What do you call a teacher with a plank of wood on his head?
Edward.

What do you call a teacher with a cat on her head?
Kitty.

What do you call a teacher with a tennis racket on her head?
Annette.

What do you call a teacher
with a seagull on his head?
Cliff.

What do you call a
teacher with
two lavatories
on her head?
Lulu.

What do you call a
teacher with a
postage stamp on
his head?
Frank.

What do you call a
teacher with
a thorn on
her head?
Rose.

What do you call a teacher with a car on his head?
Jack.

What do you call a teacher with a bus on his head?
Dead!

GEOGRAPHY TEACHER: What makes the Tower of Pisa lean?
SMART SUE: I don't suppose anybody feeds it.

RYAN: One of our teachers once lived on water for a whole year.
BRIAN: I don't think that's possible.
RYAN: It was — he was in the Navy.

SCIENCE TEACHER: Who can tell me what nitrates are?
SAMMY: I expect they're dearer than day rates, Sir.

DAVE: If we could sell our teachers we'd make lots of money!
DON: How?
DAVE: I'm not sure, but I've heard that Old Masters fetch a very high price.

TRACEY: I quite like our teachers.
STACEY: Really? When?
TRACEY: In the vacation.

TEACHER: Can you spell your name backwards, Simon?
SIMON: No, mis.

Why did the music teacher marry the school caretaker?
He swept her off her feet.

When is a teacher two teachers?
When she's beside herself.

Why did the teacher keep naughty Nigel in after school?
Because she believed that detention was better than cure.

GEOGRAPHY TEACHER: Who can name a mineral Britain imports from the USA?
SILLY SUSIE: Coca-Cola.

HERBERT: I really don't want to go to school today. Please don't make me!
HERBERT'S MOTHER: But Herbert you must go. You're the principal!

What steps do you take when the principal's angry?
Very long ones.

JANE: Have you been at this school all your life, Miss?
TEACHER: Not yet, Jane.

When is an English teacher like a judge?
When she hands out sentences.

TREVOR: I don't think our woodwork teacher likes me.
IVOR: Why's that?
TREVOR: He's teaching me how to make a coffin.

Did you hear about the cookery teacher who went on a banana diet? She didn't lose any weight but she couldn't half climb trees!

TRACEY: I know how we can find out how old our teacher is.
STACEY: How?
TRACEY: By looking at her knickers.
STACEY: Looking at her knickers! How will that help?
TRACEY: Well, my knickers have a label on them that says "Six to eight."

Why did the teacher switch on the lights?
Because his class was so dim.

Why did the bald teacher
throw away his keys?
He didn't have any locks.

Why do teachers eat biscuits?
Because they're crackers.

Why did the art teacher take a
pencil to bed?
To draw the curtains.

What goes
ha-ha-ha-clonk?
A teacher laughing
his head off.

How do you make a thin teacher fat?
Throw her off a cliff and she'll come down plump.

Where was the teacher when the lights went out?
In the dark.

Why is a drama teacher like something out of the Wild West? Because she's a stage coach.

What should a teacher take if he's feeling run down? The number of the car that hit him!

What's brown, hairy, wears dark glasses and carries a pile of books?
A coconut disguised as a teacher.

TEACHER: There were three buns in my drawer this morning and now there's only one. Can anyone explain why?
HONEST HARRY: The last one must have been hidden at the back.

Miss Haddock, the music teacher, was rather deaf. "What she needs," said one of her colleagues, "is a herring-aid."

MISS FLIVVER: Why did you become a teacher?
MISS FLUVVER: Well, I used to be a fortune-teller but I gave it up. There just wasn't any future in it.

Do teachers always snore?
No, only when they're asleep.

What's the difference between a gymnastics teacher and a duck?
One goes quick on its feet; the other goes quack with its beak.

FIRST TEACHER: How far from school do you live?
SECOND TEACHER: Ten minutes' walk if you run.

HARRY: Our German teacher can speak six different languages.
LARRY: It's a pity he speaks them all at the same time!

Why did the music teacher have a piano in her bathroom?
Because she liked playing Handel's *Water Music*.

What happened when the Scottish teacher washed his kilt?
He couldn't do a fling with it.

What did the teacher say who had jelly in one ear and custard in the other?
"You'll have to speak up, I'm a trifle deaf."

NELLIE: Our form mistress went to the West Indies for her holidays.
KELLY: Jamaica?
NELLIE: No, she went of her own accord.

EXASPERATED TEACHER: I've spent my years at this school teaching you all I know, and you know nothing!

Knock, Knock on the Library Door

Knock, knock.
Who's there?
Amanda.
Amanda who?
Amanda put the books on the library shelves.

Knock, knock.
Who's there?
Ewan.
Ewan who?
No one else, just me!

Knock, knock.
Who's there?
Sonia.
Sonia who?
Sonia me bringing my
books back.

Knock, knock.
Who's there?
Alma.
Alma who?
Alma not going to tell you!

Knock, knock.
Who's there?
Scissor.
Scissor who?
Scissor was a Roman emperor.

Knock, knock.
Who's there?
Colleen.
Colleen who?
Colleen up your desk, it's a mess.

Knock, knock.
Who's there?
Cynthia.
Cynthia who?
Cynthia been away
I've had measles.

Knock, knock.
Who's there?
Eileen.
Eileen who?
Eileen Dover and fell off my chair!

Knock, knock.
Who's there?
Enoch.
Enoch who?
Enoch and Enoch but no one answers the door!

Knock, knock.
Who's there?
Euripides.
Euripides who?
Euripides books and I shan't lend
them to you again.

Knock, knock.
Who's there?
Fitzwilliam.
Fitzwilliam who?
Fitzwilliam better than it fits me.

Knock, knock.
Who's there?
Freddie.
Freddie who?
Freddie, steady, go!

Knock, knock.
Who's there?
Gladys.
Gladys who?
Gladys Friday and
school's over for
the week!

Knock, knock.
Who's there?
Howie.
Howie who?
Howie you doing with your essay?

Knock, knock.
Who's there?
Ivan.
Ivan who?
Ivan the history prize.

Knock, knock.
Who's there?
Josette.
Josette who?
Josette down and be quiet when I'm talking.

Knock, knock.
Who's there?
Justin.
Justin who?
Justin time,
the bell's rung.

Knock, knock.
Who's there?
Liz-Anne.
Liz-Anne who?
Liz-Anne to me when
I'm talking to you!

Knock, knock.
Who's there?
Matthew.
Matthew who?
Matthew lathe hath
come undone.

Knock, knock.
Who's there?
Oscar.
Oscar who?
Oscar to go and see her form mistress.

Knock, knock.
Who's there?
Russell.
Russell who?
Russell up
some grub,
I'm starving!

Knock, knock.
Who's there?
Althea.
Althea who?
Althea after
school.

Knock, knock.
Who's there?
Beth.
Beth who?
Beth withes for your extham.

Knock, knock.
Who's there?
Denial.
Denial who?
Denial's a river in Egypt.

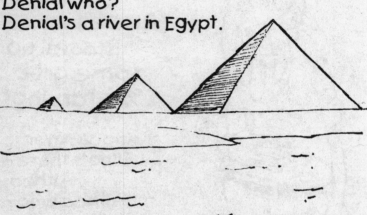

Knock, knock.
Who's there?
Reader.
Reader who?
Reader these
books next!

Crossing Siberia by I. C. Blast

To the South Pole by Anne Tarctic

Training Tigers by Claude Arm

How to Make Money by Robin Banks

Causing Insomnia by Constance Nora

Quick Snacks
by Roland
Butter

Cool Summer
Desserts
by I. Scream

Caring for
Baby by
Elsie Cries

Itchy Scalps by Dan Druff

A Bite a Day by Amos Quito

Chinese Torture by Hoo Flung Dung

Into the Classroom by Sally Forth

I Hate Math by Anne Guish

What's On Your Mind? by Eliza Wake

Aching Joints by Arthur Ritis

Moving Goods by Laurie Driver

Keep Trying by Percy Vere

Everybody Out! by Jen R.L. Strike

Good Gardening
by Anita Lawn

Growing
Vegetables
by Rosa Cabbages

The South Coast of England
by Francis Near

Corporal Punishment by Ben Dover

Raising Frogs by Lily Pond

Wait a Moment by Iza Cummin

Old Carpets by Fred Bare

Parachute
Jumping
by Hugo Furst

Portrait Painting by
Andrew Mee

The Police
Force by
Lauren Order

My Birthday by Annie Versary

Crossing the Atlantic in a
Rowing Boat by Eva Lott

Willy Pass by Betty Wont

Everlasting Torture
by L. Fire

Raising Pigs by Lena Pork

The Mystery Crime by Hugh Dunnit

Japanese Suicide by Harry Kirri

Road Safety by Luke Right and Luke Left

Train-spotting by Anna Rack

My Life as a Boxer by Esau Stars

The Poor Footballer by Mr Goal

Helping People by Linda Hand

Beachcombing
by C. Shaw

Smash and Grab
by Eva Brick

Summertime by Theresa Greene

Author Unknown
by Anne O'Nymous

Playtime by Ivor Newfootball

An Embarrassing Moment by Lucy Lastic

Advertising Pays by Bill Poster

In the Town
by Bill
Tuparea

Canoeing by River Bends

Mending Cars by Mike Annic

Knock, knock.
Who's there?
Witch.
Witch who?
Witch way
out of the
library?

Knock, knock.
Who's there?
Pickle.
Pickle who?
That's my favorite instrument!

Knock, knock.
Who's there?
Almond.
Almond who?
Almond your side in this argument!

Knock, knock.
Who's there?
Scold.
Scold who?
Scold enough to go skating!

Knock, knock.
Who's there?
Tamara.
Tamara who?
Tamara's the day of the school concert.

Knock, knock.
Who's there?
Ooze.
Ooze who?
Ooze in charge of this library?

Knock, knock.
Who's there?
Lloyd.
Lloyd who?
He lloyd to me, he said it was math but it's English!

Knock, knock.
Who's there?
Juicy.
Juicy who?
Juicy that rude drawing in this book?

Knock, knock.
Who's there?
Teacher.
Teacher who?
Teacher to copy my answers!

Knock, knock.
Who's there?
Closure.
Closure who?
Closure mouth when you're in the library.

Knock, knock.
Who's there?
Jamaica.
Jamaica who?
Jamaica mistake again?

Knock, knock.
Who's there?
Havana.
Havana who?
Havana wonderful time now school's closed.

Knock, knock.
Who's there?
Don Giovanni.
Don Giovanni who?
Don Giovanni be my friend any more?

Knock, knock.
Who's there?
Arch.
Arch who?
Sounds like you've got a cold.

Knock, knock.
Who's there?
Worzel.
Worzel who?
At the end of the corridor.

Knock, knock.
Who's there?
Radio.
Radio who?
Radio not, it's time
for school.

Knock, knock.
Who's there?
Pencil.
Pencil who?
Pencil fall down if you don't wear a belt.

Knock, knock.
Who's there?
Congo.
Congo who?
We congo on meeting behind the bookshelves.

Knock, knock.
Who's there?
Plato.
Plato who?
Plato bacon and eggs, please.

Knock, knock.
Who's there?
Egbert.
Egbert who?
Egbert no bacon, thank you.

Knock, knock.
Who's there?
Aida.
Aida who?
Aida big breakfast before I came to school.

Knock, knock.
Who's there?
Osborne.
Osborne who?
It's my birthday, Osborne today.

Knock, knock.
Who's there?
Argo.
Argo who?
Argo to piano lessons after school.

Knock, knock.
Who's there?
Jupiter.
Jupiter who?
Jupiter hurry or you'll miss the school bus.

Knock, knock.
Who's there?
Abyssinia.
Abyssinia who?
Abyssinia next term!

End of Term

What *is* the end of term?
The letter M.

When is a school like a car stopping on a hill?
When it breaks (brakes) up.

Why did the principal like to take her main holiday
in the spring?
She liked clean sheets on her bed.

KYLIE: Did you go to Spain for your holidays?
RILEY: I don't know — Dad had the tickets.

Darren went on a camping holiday with his family.
"Did the tent leak?" asked his friend Sharon.
"Only when it rained," answered Darren.

BILLY: My parents are sending me to my pen friend's for Easter.
GILLIE: Do they think you need a holiday?
BILLY: No, they think *they* need a holiday.

KEN: Won't it be wonderful when we break up for Christmas?
BEN: Do you break up for Christmas? Our family gets together!

JIMMY: Are we having Grandad and Grandma for Christmas dinner?
JIMMY'S MOM: No, dear, I think we'll have a turkey as usual.

What happens if you eat the Christmas decorations? You get tinselitis.

JENNY: What do you call a reindeer with only one eye?
KENNY: I've no idea.

**What's Santa's wife called?
Mary Christmas.**

What's Christmas called in Britain?
Yule Britannia.

FATHER: What would you like for Christmas?
JASON: I've got my eye on that lovely red bike in
the shop window on the High Street.
FATHER: Have you now? Well you'd better keep
your eye on it because you're not likely to get your
bottom on it!

AUNTIE NORA: Have a piece of my Christmas cake, dear. It's a new recipe.
JENNY: It's not very good, is it?
AUNTIE NORA: You have no taste, dear. The recipe book says quite clearly that it's delicious.

MAUREEN: Last year my uncle was arrested for doing his Christmas shopping early.
NOREEN: That's surely not against the law!
MAUREEN: It was the way he was doing it. The police caught him in a department store at 2 a.m.!

What's the difference between a teacher and a Christmas present? Everybody likes Christmas presents.

What do you call six ducks in a container on Christmas Eve?
A box of Christmas quackers.

What happens if you cross a turkey with an octopus?
Everyone can have a leg for Christmas dinner.

What did Santa give the octopus for Christmas?
Four pairs of socks.

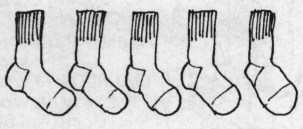

Why are Christmas trees always warm? Because they're fir trees.

Why does Santa climb down chimneys?
Because it soots him.

What does Rudolph the Red Nosed Reindeer say before he tells a joke?
"This one will sleigh you!"

Who delivers Christmas presents to pussy-cats?
Santa Claws.

Who delivers Christmas presents to private eyes?
Santa Clues.

Knock, knock.
Who's there?
Snow.
Snow who?
Snow use asking me, I can't remember.

Knock, knock.
Who's there?
Goose.
Goose who?
Goose who's
knocking at
the door!

Knock, knock.
Who's there?
Turkey.
Turkey who?
Turkey then you
can open the
door.

BILL: What are you going to be when you leave school at the end of term?
BEN: A printer.
BILL: Well, I guess you're the right type.

KEN: Did you hear what Len did when he left school?
KEITH: He went to work for a company that makes paper towels.
KEN: Does he enjoy it?
KEITH: I believe he finds it very absorbing.

Lisa went to work for a market research company. But she wasn't there long before she was sacked. You see, her vital statistics were all wrong.

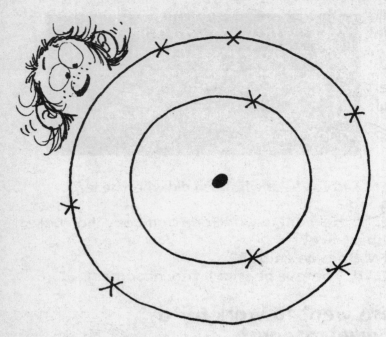

Sally was very good at physics but she didn't want to be a physicist when she left school. She said they had too many ions in the fire.

Jerry wanted to be a vicar when she left school. Her father said they wouldn't be able to put anything pastor.

Tommy wanted to be a bus driver. But his friends said that wouldn't be fair.

Milly went to work at a clock factory. When her friend asked her how she enjoyed it she replied, "Only time will tell."

Bertie got a job at a pizza factory. But it didn't pan out.

Charlie went to work at a balloon factory. Trouble was, they found it hard to keep up with inflation.

And Andrew's job as a fairgound attendant made his head spin.

BILLY: The kind of job I want is one where every day is a day off.

TILLY: If only it were possible!

BILLY: Look at it this way. There are 365 days in a year — 366 in a leap year. The working day is eight hours long — a third of a day — so that makes 122 whole days a year. No one works on Sundays so that's 52 days off, leaving 70. Take off two weeks' holiday and you've got 56. Then take off four bank holidays, leaving 52. But no one works on Saturdays, so take away 52 Saturdays and you've got every day off!

SARAH: I'm going to sunbathe on my holiday. I love the sun.

SUSIE: Oh, so do I. I could lie in the sun all day and all night.

Lizzie got a bad case of sunburn. When she complained how sore it was, her brother remarked, "Well, I guess you basked for it."

Donald once stayed up all night trying to work out what happened to the sun when it set. It finally dawned on him.

Darren was showing Sharon his holiday photos. She admired all the scenery and the people. Then Darren showed her a picture of him having a donkey ride on the beach. "Who's that on your back?" asked Sharon.

Why can you never starve
on a beach?
Because of all the sand
which is there.

What did the sea
say to the beach?
Nothing, it just
waved.

Why did the lobster
blush?
Because the
seaweed.

Kylie and Riley were talking about their forthcoming summer holidays. "Last year," said Kylie, "my brother and I took turns to bury each other in the sand." "Yes, but what about this year?" interrupted Riley. "I was coming to that," said Kylie. "This year we're going back to try to find him."

What did one rock pool say to another?
"Show us your mussels."

Why was the seaweed embarrassed?
Because it saw the ship's bottom.

What sits on the seabed and shivers?
A nervous wreck.

The trouble with the end of term is that it's when the school reports go out.
When Sheila's dad got hers he said, "Why is your report so poor? Your teacher seems to think you're really stupid."
"Well, she would," replied Sheila. "You see, she's a graduate."

What is a school report? A poison pen letter from a teacher.

After Cheryl's mom got her report, she told Cheryl
she really must work harder.
"Hard work never killed anyone," she said.
"And I don't want to be the first!" retorted Cheryl.

MOM: This report says you are very careless in
your appearance.
MINNIE: Really?
MOM: Yes, it says you only appear at school about
once a week.

How can you make the dumbo in your class laugh
at the beginning of term?
Tell him a joke at the end of the previous term.

Knock, knock.
Who's there?
Norma Lee.
Norma Lee who?
Norma Lee I go to school but today is the first day of the holidays!

How do schoolchildren in Lapland dress in the Christmas holidays?
Quickly!

What did the Eskimo children sing when one of their class was leaving school?
"Freeze a jolly good fellow."

The careers teacher was interviewing school-leavers just before the end of term.
"What kind of job do you think you'd like, Mike?" he asked one boy.
"One with lots of openings," replied Mike.
"How about being a doorman?"

DAVE: I'd like to be an archeologist.
MAVE: What's that?
DAVE: Someone whose career is in ruins.

Margie went to work in a grocer's shop. She was 1.6 meters tall and she took size seven shoes. What did she weigh? Ham and cheese.

Lester was the school karate champion and when he left he joined the army. He didn't last long, though. Every time he saluted he ended up in hospital.

Miss Gossage was asking her pupils what they wanted to do when they left school.
"What will you do, Lionel, when you're as big as your father?" she asked one boy.
"Go on a diet," was the crisp reply.

Jim and his mom and dad went out in the rain on their holiday but only two of them got their hair wet. Why?
Jim's dad was completely bald!

Just before they broke up for the Christmas holidays, the school went to a special service in the local church. Afterwards their teacher asked if they had enjoyed it, and if they had all behaved properly.

"Oh yes," replied one little girl. "And we were ever so good. When someone came round with a plate of money we all said no thank you."

MR BROWN: What's your son going to be when he's passed all his exams and left school?
MR GREEN: At the rate he's going, a senior citizen.

Daft Donald was telling his friends how they forecast the weather when they were staying in their holiday cottage in Scotland.
"We used a piece of string," he explained.
"How?" asked a friend.
"Outside the window," explained Donald.
"And how did that tell what the weather was?" persisted the friend.
"If it moved, it was windy; if it got wet, it was raining," answered Donald.

In the holidays a teacher went into a shoe shop and asked for some crocodile shoes.
"Certainly, madam," replied the assistant. "How big is your crocodile?"

Ben's sister, Samantha, wanted to be an actress when she left school.
"Is she pretty?" asked Bill.
"Let's just say she has a perfect face for radio," answered Ben.

Why did Sally want to work in a bank?
She'd heard there was money in it.

MR CHINN: I hear your daughter became a writer when she left school. Does she write for money?
MR KNOWS: Yes, with almost every letter we get!

Tina went to work in a florist's but she got the sack. Her friend Gina asked what had happened.
"I mixed up the cards in the bouquets," she answered. "One bouquet was going to a wedding and I put a card on it saying 'With deepest sympathy.' The other flowers were going to a funeral and I put on a card saying 'Hope you'll be happy in your new home'!"

JIM: How do you get to be a coroner?
TIM: You have to take a stiff exam.

Brian went to be a telephone engineer and spent his time mending faults on the line. It drove him up the pole.

LIONEL: There's only one sure-fire way to make money.
LAURA: What's that?
LIONEL: I might have known you wouldn't know!

When Harry went for a job interview the boss said, "We work very early hours here. I take it that wouldn't bother you?"
"Oh, no," replied Harry. "You can't stop early enough for me!"

But breaking up doesn't necessarily mean leaving school. A lot of us have to go back again ...

TEACHER: Did you miss school while you were on holiday?
SUSIE: Not a bit!

And, finally ...

How do you get to be
the most advanced pupil
in the school?
Sit in the front row!

CHILDREN'S BOOKS AVAILABLE FROM
ROBINSON PUBLISHING

The Biggest Joke Book in the World *Tom & Matt Keegan* £6.99
All the jokes you will ever need to know.

The Joke Museum
  Sandy Ransford £3.99
A collection of the finest, funniest
and oldest jokes in the world.

The Big Bad Joke Book
  Zig and Zag £3.99
Zig and Zag present over
1,000 fantastic jokes.

1001 Knock Knock Jokes
  Jasmine Birtles £3.99
All the old favorites as well as
hilarious new ones.

**The Ultimate Book of
Unforgettable Creepy Crawly
Jokes**
  Liz Hughes £6.99
Jokes about everything from slugs
and mosquitoes, bees and bats to
creepy ghouls and witches' cats.

1001 Animal Quacker Jokes
  Jasmine Birtles £3.99
There are jokes in here for every
animal you can imagine – and some you can't!

The Biggest Book of Stupid Jokes in the Universe *David Mostyn* £6.99
Jam-packed with a spectacular selection of the most incredibly stupid – but
hilariously funny – jokes.

Big Bad Classroom Jokes *Sandy Ransford* £3.99
All the very best jokes to be invented in the classroom.

The Puzzle Factory *Sue Preston* £3.99
The ultimate puzzle challenge, which will keep even the brightest minds occupied
for hours.

The Biggest Puzzle Book in the World £5.99
Nutty word games, mad mazes, codes to crack and hundreds more puzzle
challenges.

Dance Stories   *Felicity Trotman*   £4.99
Wonderful collection of exciting, glamorous and romantic stories about the world
of dance.

Fantasy Stories   *Mike Ashley*   £4.99
Some of the best fantasy stories of the century. Many have been written especially
for this book, others are classics.

True Mystery Stories   *Finn Bevan*   £4.99
Collection of thirty tales based on the world's most fascinating unexplained
phenomena.

True Sea Stories   *Paul Aston*   £4.99
Tales of mystery, crime and piracy, sunken treasure, races won and lost, and
silent, deadly beasts beneath the waves.

True Horror Stories   *Terrance Dicks*   £4.99
More than thirty accounts of truly terrifying experiences, including the horror of
a plane crash and of being trapped underground.

True Survival Stories   *Anthony Masters*   £4.99
Gripping tales of survival against all the odds, including Apollo 13, the Andes
plane crash, and many more.

Robinson books are available from all good bookshops or can be ordered direct
from the publisher. Just tick the title you want and fill in the form below.

Robinson Publishing Ltd, PO Box 11, Falmouth, Cornwall TR10 9EN
Tel: +44(0) 1326 374900 Fax: +44(0) 1326 374888 Email: books@Barni.avel.co.uk

UK/BFPO customers please allow £1.00 for p&p for the first book, plus 50p for the second,
plus 30p for each additional book up to a maximum charge of £3.

Overseas customers (inc. Ireland) please allow £2.00 for the first book, plus £1.00 for the
second, plus 50p for each additional book.

Please send me the titles ticked above.

NAME (Block letters) ....

ADDRESS ....

....POSTCODE ....

I enclose a cheque/PO (payable to Robinson Publishing Ltd) for ....
I wish to pay by Switch/Credit Card

....Card Expiry Date ....